Bill Granger Easy

Bill Granger Easy

Photography by Mikkel Vang

 Collins

Easy does it

I always imagined life was going to slow down and get easier – once the children were out of nappies; once the business was up and running. But it seems to speed up every day, doesn't it. Perhaps by now I should be into my Elizabeth David phase, writing recipes that need a free weekend to hunt down and roast a wild boar? But, instead of even growing my own vegetables, I still find myself with barely enough time to race around the supermarket and buy them. It's all too easy to forget – in this fast-paced wind tunnel of life – that true happiness comes with relationships, and relationships thrive on good food. As my mum likes to say, 'Life's too short to stuff a mushroom.' So invite your friends over and cook them something delicious, but EASY.

Piece of chicken

Chicken is the great traveller, the easy-going backpacker of the food world, who happily joins in with every culture and is keen to make friends with every flavour she meets: from Thai lemongrass to French thyme, Mexican chipotles to Tunisian harissa. In just one generation chicken has become our favourite go-to meat for almost every meal (certainly in my house, anyway). For my father's generation, roast chook was served with great fanfare for Christmas lunch; this week, I'll probably stir-fry, pan-fry, curry, roast, poach or toss it into a salad two or three times to feed the family.

CHILLI CHICKEN + SKORDALIA OK, you've spotted it: this is really chicken and mash – but I make no apologies for my double-chilli chicken with garlicky skordalia.

1 red chilli, halved and sliced
1 teaspoon dried chilli flakes
1 garlic clove, crushed
4 tablespoons olive oil
1.5kg chicken legs
handful pea shoots or watercress
lemon wedges

Place the fresh chilli, chilli flakes, garlic and oil in a bowl and mix to combine. Cut deep slashes in the chicken pieces and rub the marinade over the skin and into the slashes. Place in an ovenproof tray or tin, cover with cling film and leave to chill in the fridge for at least 30 minutes.

Preheat the oven to 200°C/gas mark 6. Roast the chicken for 45–50 minutes, or until cooked through and golden. Remove from the oven and set aside in a warm place to rest for 10–15 minutes. Serve with the skordalia, pea shoots and lemon wedges. **SERVES 4**

SKORDALIA

1kg potatoes, peeled and
  cut into large chunks
2 tablespoons olive oil
2 garlic cloves, crushed
160ml soured cream

Place the potatoes in a large saucepan of cold water. Bring to the boil over high heat and cook for about 20 minutes, or until tender when pierced with a knife. Drain the water off the potatoes and return to the stove over low heat for a minute to remove any excess water. Remove from the stove and mash thoroughly, then add the olive oil, garlic and soured cream. Season well with sea salt and freshly ground black pepper and beat until smooth.

'When I was growing up my aunt always told me, "Never serve chicken on the bone at dinner parties, or your guests will be forced to use their fingers." Today, our friends seem very happy to throw down the knife and fork and gnaw away.'

ROAST CHICKEN SALAD + CHIVE MAYONNAISE Making your own mayo always tends to impress people, even though it only takes two minutes and a blender. You can liven up shop-bought whole egg mayo with a little lemon juice and sea salt.

1kg boneless chicken thighs,
  skin on
1 lemon, halved
½ ciabatta, torn into chunks
2 tablespoons olive oil
4 eggs
1 small iceberg lettuce,
  cut into wedges
handful celery leaves
3 celery sticks, cut into
  5cm-long batons
finely chopped chives, to serve

Preheat the oven to 220°C/gas mark 7. Place the chicken on an oven tray lined with baking paper, squeeze lemon juice over the top and season with sea salt and freshly ground black pepper. Roast for 35–45 minutes or until the skin is golden. About 10 minutes before the chicken should be ready, toss the bread in the oil in a bowl, season well and then add the bread to the baking tray.

Meanwhile, bring a small saucepan of water to a simmer over high heat. Add the eggs, reduce the heat and simmer gently for 6 minutes. Drain and plunge into cold water. When cool enough to handle, peel and slice into thick rounds.

Take the tray from the oven. Remove the bread and set the chicken aside to rest in a warm place for 5–10 minutes. Slice the chicken and toss with the bread, lettuce, celery leaves and batons. Divide into serving bowls and dress with the soft-boiled eggs and chive mayonnaise. Sprinkle with chopped chives and freshly ground black pepper. **SERVES 4–6**

CHIVE MAYONNAISE

2 egg yolks
1 tablespoon lemon juice
250ml light-flavoured oil
2 tablespoons finely
  chopped chives

Use a blender to blend the egg yolks, a pinch of sea salt and lemon juice until well combined. With the motor running, slowly add the oil, 1 tablespoon at a time, until the mixture is thick and creamy. If you find your mayonnaise splits or curdles, the addition of a little boiling water can bring it together. Stir through the chives just before serving.

PAPRIKA AND CORIANDER ROASTED CHICKEN This roast chicken comes out of the oven in a sea of wonderful vibrant juices. Mop them up with bread or rice.

1.5kg chicken legs
2 lemons, 1 cut into
   8 wedges and 1 juiced
2 tablespoons olive oil
2 teaspoons coriander seeds,
   crushed
1 teaspoon paprika
4 tablespoons soy sauce
2 garlic cloves, crushed
3 onions, cut into thin wedges
steamed rice (see page 35)

Season the chicken pieces with sea salt and freshly ground black pepper and place in a dish. In a bowl mix together the lemon juice, oil, coriander seeds, paprika, soy sauce and garlic to make a marinade. Pour over the chicken and rub into the skin. Cover and place in the fridge for 30 minutes.

Preheat the oven to 200°C/gas mark 6. Place the onion and lemon wedges on the bottom of a baking tray to form a bed. Place the chicken pieces on top and pour over the marinade.

Roast for 35 minutes or until the chicken is cooked through, basting occasionally to prevent the chicken drying out. Serve with steamed rice. **SERVES 4-6**

LIGHT BUTTER CHICKEN I'm far too vain to be able to enjoy butter chicken these days. This version uses yoghurt to keep my arteries (and conscience) a bit clearer.

2 tablespoons light-flavoured oil
1 large onion, finely chopped
2 tablespoons tandoori
   curry paste
750g skinless chicken thighs,
   cut into 2cm chunks
400g tin chopped tomatoes
125ml chicken stock
100g cashew nuts
125g thick Greek yoghurt
1 tablespoon lemon juice
1 tablespoon soft brown sugar
steamed basmati rice
   (see page 35)
1 white onion, roughly chopped
handful coriander,
   roughly chopped
lime wedges

Heat the oil in a large wok or frying pan over medium–high heat. Add the onion and cook, stirring occasionally, for 6–8 minutes, or until golden and softened. Add the curry paste and cook for a further 1–2 minutes, stirring, until fragrant. Add the chicken and cook, stirring to coat, for 2–3 minutes. Add the tomatoes and stock and stir to combine. Bring to a simmer, reduce heat to low and cook gently for 15 minutes, or until the chicken is cooked through.

Meanwhile, blitz the cashew nuts in a food processor until finely ground. Add to the chicken and simmer gently for a further 5 minutes, or until the sauce has thickened. Remove from the heat and stir through the yoghurt, lemon juice and sugar.

Serve the curry with steamed rice, dressed with onion, coriander and a squeeze of lime juice. **SERVES 4**

SPICED CHICKEN WRAPS + MANGO CHUTNEY This is quick, but to make it ridiculously speedy, marinate the chicken in two tablespoons tandoori paste and serve with a bought mango chutney. There's absolutely no excuse for takeaway.

310g thick Greek yoghurt
2 teaspoons paprika
1 teaspoon ground cumin
1 teaspoon ground coriander
1 teaspoon turmeric
2 large garlic cloves, crushed
3cm piece ginger,
   peeled and grated
1kg chicken breast fillets,
   flattened with a mallet
   or rolling pin
½ long cucumber,
   cut into wedges
½ red onion, thinly sliced
1 red chilli, sliced
handful coriander and mint leaves
1 lemon, cut into wedges
wholemeal flat bread, toasted
natural yoghurt

Mix the Greek yoghurt with the spices, garlic and ginger in a bowl large enough to hold all the chicken fillets. Season well with sea salt and freshly ground black pepper, add the chicken and mix with your hands to coat. Cover and place in the fridge to marinate for 30 minutes.

Place the cucumber, red onion and chilli in a bowl and toss gently to combine. Preheat a barbecue or chargrill pan on high heat. Remove the chicken from the marinade and cook for 4–5 minutes on each side, until cooked through.

Slice the chicken and serve with separate bowls of the mango chutney, vegetables, torn herbs, lemon wedges, flat bread and yoghurt and let everyone make their own wraps. **SERVES 4-6**

MANGO CHUTNEY

3 mangoes, peeled
3 garlic cloves, chopped
1½ tablespoons grated ginger
1 red chilli, chopped
1 tablespoon coriander seeds
½ teaspoon turmeric
2 tablespoons olive oil
1 cinnamon stick
1 teaspoon sea salt
100g caster sugar
125ml cider vinegar

Cut the mango flesh away from the stone and chop into a small dice. Place the garlic, ginger, chilli, coriander seeds and turmeric in a mortar and pestle and crush to a paste.

Heat the oil in a saucepan over medium heat. Add the spice paste and cinnamon stick and fry for 1 minute, or until fragrant. Add the diced mango, salt, sugar and vinegar and cook for 30 minutes, until thick and syrupy. Set aside to cool.

CHICKEN PAILLARD WITH SPRING ONIONS AND PROSCIUTTO The secret to well-cooked, juicy chicken breast is to slice it thin and cook it quick.

4 chicken breast fillets, cut
  into 3 pieces lengthways
1 tablespoon olive oil
1 lemon, sliced
1 tablespoon unsalted butter
4 thin slices prosciutto,
  roughly torn
4 spring onions, finely sliced
310ml chicken stock
2 tablespoons crème fraîche
2 courgettes, cut into
  chunks and steamed

Bash out the chicken pieces until nicely thin. Drizzle with the oil and season with sea salt and freshly ground black pepper. Place a frying pan over high heat and add the chicken pieces and lemon slices. Sear for 2 minutes on one side and then turn over and sear the other side for 30 seconds. Remove from the pan and cover to keep warm.

Reduce the heat to medium and add the butter to melt. Fry the prosciutto for 1 minute, or until lightly browned. Add the onions and cook for 30 seconds, then pour in the chicken stock and let bubble for a few minutes until thickened slightly. Remove from heat, stir in the crème fraîche and season well. Divide the chicken into serving plates, pour over the sauce and serve with the steamed courgettes. **SERVES 4**

MOROCCAN CHICKEN PIES At the risk of sounding like a Stepford Wife (or Husband!), always make double the quantity and put some away in the freezer.

50g plain flour
1 teaspoon ground cinnamon
1 teaspoon turmeric
750g skinless chicken thighs,
  cut into 3cm dice
2 tablespoons olive oil
1 large onion, finely chopped
2 garlic cloves, crushed
2 teaspoons grated ginger
500g butternut squash,
  peeled, deseeded and
  cut into small chunks
100g dried apricots,
  roughly chopped
100g pitted green olives
375ml chicken stock
1 tablespoon preserved lemon
  rind, finely chopped
375g block ready-made
  butter puff pastry
1 egg yolk, lightly beaten

Preheat the oven to 180°C/gas mark 4. Combine the flour, cinnamon and turmeric in a bowl and season with sea salt and freshly ground black pepper. Toss the chicken to coat, shaking off any excess flour. Place the oil in a large, deep frying pan over medium–high heat. Add the onion, garlic and ginger and cook, stirring occasionally, for 5–6 minutes, until soft. Increase heat to high, add the chicken and cook for 2–3 minutes, until the chicken is lightly browned.

Add the squash, apricots, olives, stock and preserved lemon, bring to the boil, then reduce heat to low and simmer for 10 minutes. Remove from the heat, season to taste and set aside in the fridge until cold.

You will need six 250ml ramekins or ovenproof dishes. Roll out the pastry on a lightly floured surface until about 4mm thick. Using one dish upside down as a guide, cut out 6 rounds of pastry 1cm larger than the circumference of the dish. Spoon the chicken filling into each dish, brush the rim with egg yolk and cover with the pastry lid, pushing down lightly around the rim to seal. Brush the pie tops with more egg yolk and bake for 35–40 minutes, until golden brown. **SERVES 6**

Fillet of fish

Fish has found itself swimming through a confusing, watery battleground recently. We've all learnt the importance of brain-charging, mood-lifting Omega 3, and I've certainly discovered that my waistline loves fish three times a week. No dinner is quicker to put on the table than a fillet of fish, it literally takes minutes to cook. Now we're weighing up these plus points against the environmental dangers of overfishing. I try to buy fish that's from sustainable fisheries and keep up with current developments, but I'm not giving it up just yet; not while I still have my old jeans to fit into.

TANDOORI FISH + CUCUMBER TOMATO SALAD My recipe says to marinate this for 15 minutes. In my life, and probably in yours, this ends up being a rushed three minutes. Try to do as I say, not as I do. Or do your best!

3 tablespoons thick
  Greek yoghurt
3 tablespoons tandoori
  curry paste
1 tablespoon lemon juice
2 garlic cloves, crushed
1 tablespoon grated ginger
4 white fish fillets, skinned
  (about 180g each)
lime pickle (shop bought)
1 lime, cut into wedges

CUCUMBER TOMATO SALAD

½ long cucumber,
  roughly chopped
2 tomatoes, roughly chopped
2 tablespoons thick
  Greek yoghurt
2 tablespoons roughly chopped
  mint leaves
1 teaspoon cumin seeds,
  toasted and lightly crushed

Preheat a grill to high. Mix together the yoghurt, tandoori paste, lemon juice, garlic and ginger in a bowl. Add the fish and coat well. Cover and leave to marinate in the fridge for 15 minutes.

Lift the fish from the marinade and place in a single layer on an oven tray lined with foil, keeping space between each fillet. Grill for 3–4 minutes, or until just cooked. Serve with the cucumber tomato salad, lime pickle and lime wedges. **SERVES 4**

Place the cucumber, tomato and yoghurt in a bowl and stir gently to combine. Add the mint leaves and scatter with cumin seeds.

HOISIN MARINATED SALMON + CHILLI SOY TENDERSTEM BROCCOLI The combination of hoisin and fish works here because of the meatiness of the salmon.

2 tablespoons soy sauce
2 tablespoons hoisin sauce
1 tablespoon rice wine vinegar
1 tablespoon olive oil
1 tablespoon lemon juice
2cm piece ginger, grated
2 garlic cloves, finely chopped
1 red chilli, roughly chopped
4 salmon fillets, skinned
   (about 175g each)
steamed rice (see recipe below)

Stir together the soy sauce, hoisin sauce, vinegar, olive oil, lemon juice, ginger, garlic and chilli in a large bowl. Add the salmon and leave to marinate in the fridge for at least 15 minutes and up to 1 hour.

Preheat the oven to 220°C/gas mark 7. Arrange the salmon fillets in a single layer on a roasting tray lined with baking paper. Roast for 15 minutes (the fish should still be pink in the centre). Serve with chilli soy tenderstem broccoli and steamed jasmine rice. **SERVES 4**

CHILLI SOY TENDERSTEM BROCCOLI

100ml soy sauce
2 tablespoons Chinese
   black rice vinegar
2 tablespoons light-flavoured oil
1 red chilli, finely chopped
1½ teaspoons caster sugar
1 tablespoon lime juice
500g tenderstem broccoli,
   trimmed

Place the soy sauce, vinegar, 1 tablespoon of the oil, chilli, sugar and lime juice in a bowl and stir well. Tip the remaining oil into a saucepan of boiling salted water and blanch the broccoli for 30 seconds, until tender but still crisp and bright green.

Drain and arrange on a warm serving platter. Pour over the dressing and serve immediately.

STEAMED RICE

400g long-grain white,
   Jasmine or basmati rice
600ml water

Rinse the rice in a fine sieve, preferably until the water runs clear, and drain well. Put the rice and water in a large saucepan with a tight-fitting lid. Bring to the boil, put the lid on the pan, reduce the heat to low and cook for 12 minutes. Turn the heat off and leave to stand for 10 minutes.

Do not remove the lid at any time during the cooking and standing process. Serve immediately. **SERVES 4**

'If you're not a good washer-upper — and I'm certainly not — this is the way to go: a main course cooked in a paper parcel, leaving no pots or pans to scrub. I'm a big fan of minimalist cooking.'

BAKED FISH WITH CAPERS, POTATOES AND LEMON Dinner party perfection: no pan wrangling while entertaining your guests; no lingering smell of fried fish.

300g new potatoes,
   skin on, finely sliced
3 tablespoons olive oil
1 tablespoon capers
1 garlic clove, finely chopped
4 white fish fillets, skinned
   (about 180g each)
1 lemon, sliced
large handful mixed herbs
   (tarragon, flat-leaf parsley,
   chervil, fennel or dill),
   roughly chopped

Preheat the oven and a baking tray to 200°C/gas mark 6. Bring a large saucepan of salted water to the boil and cook the potatoes until just tender, about 5–10 minutes depending on the thickness of the slices. Drain well.

Mix the olive oil, capers and garlic in a small bowl and season well with sea salt and feshly ground black pepper. Lay out 4 sheets of baking paper, about 30cm x 40cm each. Divide the potato slices among the sheets, making a rectangular bed roughly the same size as the fish in the centre of each one. Drizzle with half the oil mixture, then top with the fish fillets and lemon slices. Scatter over the mixed herbs and finish with the remaining oil mixture. Wrap up each fish parcel, tucking the ends under. (Secure the parcels with foil if you like.) Transfer the parcels to the preheated tray and bake for 12–15 minutes, or until just cooked through. **SERVES 4**

SPANISH FISH STEW We're always hearing about that miraculous Mediterranean Omega 3 diet. This is it in a bowl. We're going to live forever...

2 tablespoons olive oil
1 large onion, thinly sliced
1 celery stick, chopped
2 garlic cloves, crushed
1 teaspoon paprika
1 large red pepper,
   cut into strips
250ml white wine
400g tin chopped tomatoes
pinch cayenne pepper
few strands saffron
400ml fish stock
600g firm white fish fillets,
   skinned and cut into chunks
400g tin chickpeas,
   drained and rinsed
large handful flat-leaf parsley
lemon wedges

Heat the olive oil in a large heavy-based pan over medium–low heat. Add the onion and celery and cook, stirring occasionally, for 5 minutes or until the onion is translucent. Add the garlic, paprika and red pepper and cook, stirring, for 3 minutes more until fragrant and the pepper is starting to soften. Pour in the wine and continue cooking until reduced slightly.

Add the tomatoes, cayenne, saffron, fish stock and a pinch of sea salt and simmer for 10 minutes, stirring frequently. Add the fish and simmer for 3 minutes, or until the fish is just tender. Add the chickpeas and cook for a further 2–3 minutes. Season with sea salt and freshly ground black pepper. Serve in individual bowls with the parsley and lemon wedges. **SERVES 4**

YELLOW FISH CURRY + COCONUT RICE Curry paste is ludicrously easy to make and tastes vastly better than the bought variety. Place the leftover paste in a sterilised jar in the fridge and use it within a week.

2 tablespoons light-flavoured oil
2 tablespoons yellow curry paste
  (recipe below or shop bought)
1 teaspoon ground cumin
1 teaspoon ground coriander
½ teaspoon turmeric
400ml tin coconut milk
1 tablespoon fish sauce
1 tablespoon soft brown sugar
6 kaffir lime leaves
300g green beans, trimmed
  and cut into 3cm lengths
600g thick white fish fillets,
  skinned, cut into
  bite-sized pieces

Place a large wok or non-stick frying pan over medium–high heat. Add the oil and, when hot, add the curry paste, cumin, coriander and turmeric. Fry for 1 minute, stirring constantly. Stir in the coconut milk, fish sauce, sugar and lime leaves, then add the beans with 50ml water. Bring to a simmer and cook for 3 minutes.

Drop the fish gently into the simmering curry and cook for 3–5 minutes, or until the fish is just cooked. Season with a little more fish sauce if liked. Serve with the coconut rice. **SERVES 4**

COCONUT RICE

200ml coconut cream
400g white long-grain rice

Combine the coconut cream, rice and 375ml water in a medium saucepan. Cover and bring to the boil over high heat, then reduce heat to low and simmer gently for 12–14 minutes, or until the liquid has been absorbed. Set aside with the lid on for a further 10 minutes. **SERVES 4**

YELLOW CURRY PASTE

1 teaspoon white peppercorns
1 teaspoon coriander seeds
½ teaspoon cumin seeds
1 teaspoon sea salt
2 teaspoons turmeric
1 teaspoon curry powder
1 lemongrass stalk, white
  part only, chopped
1 teaspoon dried chilli flakes
1 yellow pepper, chopped
1 small red onion, chopped
5 garlic cloves, chopped
3cm piece ginger,
  peeled and chopped
2 tablespoons light-flavoured oil

Heat a small saucepan over medium heat. Add the peppercorns, coriander and cumin seeds and toast for 1–2 minutes, or until fragrant. Place the toasted spices and the remaining ingredients in a food processor and pulse to a paste. Store in a sterilised container in the fridge for up to a week.
MAKES ABOUT 250G

PAN-FRIED SALMON WITH CUCUMBER AND LEMON SALSA The crispy skin is my favourite part of the salmon. The secret is a very hot pan and lots of sea salt.

4 salmon fillets, skin on
 (about 175g each)
4 tablespoons olive oil
1 long cucumber, halved
 lengthways, deseeded
 and thinly sliced
1 lemon, peeled and segmented
1 small red chilli, finely chopped
small handful chopped mint
½ teaspoon caster sugar
2 garlic cloves, finely sliced
250g baby spinach leaves
sesame oil, to drizzle

Heat a large frying pan over high heat until hot. Brush the salmon with 2 tablespoons of the olive oil and season all over with sea salt and freshly ground black pepper. Sear the salmon for 2–3 minutes on each side (this will be rare) and set aside.

For the salsa, combine the cucumber, lemon, chilli, mint and sugar in a bowl and season well. Set aside.

Heat the remaining oil in a frying pan over medium–high heat. Add the garlic and fry for about 1 minute, until light golden. Add the spinach and cook for 1–2 minutes, or until wilted.

Divide the spinach among the serving plates and top with a piece of salmon and the salsa. Drizzle with sesame oil and serve immediately. **SERVES 4**

CHUNKY FISHCAKES These are made with cubed fish and torn bread. You can definitely see what's in them, which is the way I like my food.

500g firm white fish fillets,
 skinned and cut into 1cm dice
200g ciabatta, torn into
 small pieces (about 1cm)
4 tablespoons mayonnaise,
 plus extra for dipping
1 egg, beaten
1 green chilli, finely chopped
3 tablespoons coriander, chopped
1 tablespoon finely grated ginger
4 spring onions, sliced
60ml light-flavoured oil
lime wedges
2 heads chicory,
 broken into leaves
dried chilli flakes

Place the fish in a mixing bowl with the torn bread, mayonnaise, egg, chilli, coriander, ginger and spring onion. Season well with sea salt and freshly ground black pepper and mix together with your hands. Squeeze the mixture tightly to form 16 patties. Cover and refrigerate for at least 30 minutes. (This can be done in advance and the patties chilled overnight.)

Heat the oil in a frying pan over medium–high heat. Fry the fishcakes in batches for 3 minutes on each side or until crisp, keeping them warm until all patties are cooked. Serve immediately with mayonnaise, lime wedges, chicory leaves and a sprinkle of chilli flakes. **SERVES 4**

Slab of steak

I've been through my vegetarian phase – I lasted almost two weeks before I started to fret about iron deficiency. I suspect there's a bit of Argentinian blood in me somewhere: I like my steaks thick-sliced and quickly seared, so they're red and very juicy in the centre. I've noticed the English slice their steaks thinner than us Aussies, but I'm putting on a brave face. And England has its compensations: I recently visited the Sandringham Estate, met the special Royal cows and was served a beefy lunch. So, you could say, I've shared a steak with the Queen. That's my story anyway and I'm sticking to it.

MARINATED STEAK ROLLS + BARBECUE SAUCE I'd pit this against all-comers as the best steak sauce ever. It's excellent Saturday afternoon footy-watching fodder.

4 tablespoons soy sauce
1 tablespoon soft brown sugar
2 garlic cloves, crushed
1 teaspoon sesame oil
1 teaspoon grated ginger
3 sirloin steaks, 2.5cm thick
  (about 350g each)
handful fine strips carrot and
  daikon, cut on a mandolin
handful coriander and mint leaves
3 baguettes, cut into
  10cm lengths

Place the soy sauce, 1 tablespoon water, sugar, garlic, sesame oil, ginger and a pinch of freshly ground black pepper in a bowl and stir to combine. Rub over the steaks and marinate in the fridge for 15 minutes.

Preheat a barbecue or chargrill pan to high heat. Sear the steaks for 3 minutes on each side (this will cook your steak medium–rare), then cover and set aside to rest in a warm place for 5 minutes.

Slice the steak and serve on a platter with the barbecue sauce, a bowl of mixed carrot and daikon with herbs and the baguettes, for everyone to make their own steak rolls. Alternatively, make up the rolls and serve on a big platter. **SERVES 6**

BARBECUE SAUCE

100ml hoisin sauce
3 tablespoons rice wine vinegar
1 tablespoon fish sauce
3 tablespoons soy sauce
1 tablespoon honey
4 garlic cloves, crushed
2 teaspoons grated ginger
¼ teaspoon five spice powder
110g granulated sugar

Place all the ingredients in a small saucepan over medium–high heat and stir until the sugar dissolves. Simmer for a further 5 minutes, stirring occasionally. Remove from heat and cool to room temperature.

STEAK SALAD + CHIMICHURRI DRESSING The sauce of fresh herbs means this steak is as far from the stereotypical artery-clogging business lunch as you can get.

4 sirloin steaks, 2.5cm thick
 (about 350g each)
1 tablespoon olive oil
120g micro leaf salad
4 cooked beetroot, roughly cut
2 avocados, halved,
 stoned and sliced

Heat a frying pan on high heat. Brush the steaks with the oil and season with sea salt and freshly ground black pepper. Cook for 2 minutes on each side (for rare), or to your liking. Rest the steaks for 5 minutes before serving with the chimichurri dressing, micro leaf salad, beetroot wedges and avocado. **SERVES 4**

CHIMICHURRI DRESSING

Combine all the ingredients in a bowl and season well. Set aside until needed.

2 tablespoons chopped
 flat-leaf parsley
2 tablespoons chopped coriander
2 teaspoons chopped oregano
1 garlic clove, crushed
1 green chilli, chopped
2 tablespoons white wine vinegar
½ teaspoon caster sugar
80ml extra-virgin olive oil
2 tablespoons lime juice

BEEF, MUSHROOM AND MANGETOUT STIR-FRY Here's something to do with those fancy expensive mushrooms you bought at the farmers' market.

5 tablespoons hoisin sauce
1 tablespoon soy sauce
1 teaspoon chilli sauce
¼ teaspoon five spice powder
3 tablespoons light-flavoured oil
600g sirloin steak,
 fat removed, thinly sliced
1 tablespoon grated ginger
300g mixed mushrooms (shiitake,
 button, enoki), thickly sliced
200g mangetout
600g fresh rice noodles,
 warmed in hot water
2 spring onions, sliced
handful coriander,
 roughly chopped

In a bowl stir together the hoisin, soy and chilli sauces with the five spice powder and set aside.

Heat a wok or large frying pan over high heat. Add 1 tablespoon of the oil and, when hot, add half the beef and stir-fry for 1–2 minutes to seal and brown. Remove from the wok and repeat with another tablespoon of oil and the remaining beef. Remove. Add the final tablespoon of oil and stir-fry the ginger and mushrooms for 2 minutes. Add the mangetout and stir-fry for a further 2 minutes. Return the beef to the wok, tip in the sauce and cook for another minute to warm through.

Drain the noodles and divide among serving bowls. Top with the beef stir-fry, spring onion and coriander. **SERVES 4**

VIETNAMESE BEEF CURRY The combination of Indian curry powder, fish sauce and coconut milk is traditionally Vietnamese. Show off your knowledge of the country's heritage by serving it with French bread.

1kg rump steak,
  cut into 4cm cubes
1 onion, halved and finely sliced
4 garlic cloves, crushed
3cm piece ginger, grated
2 tablespoons hot Madras
  curry powder
1 teaspoon turmeric
1 tablespoon caster sugar
2 tablespoons light-flavoured oil
500ml beef stock
3 tablespoons fish sauce
2 carrots, peeled
  and cut into chunks
500g potatoes, peeled
  and cut into chunks
250ml coconut milk
1 long baguette

Preheat the oven to 160°C/gas mark 3. Toss the beef with the onion, garlic, ginger, curry powder, turmeric and sugar and season well with sea salt and freshly ground black pepper. Cover and marinate in the fridge for 15 minutes.

Heat the oil in a large shallow casserole dish over medium heat. Add the beef, in batches, and cook until browned. Return all the meat to the dish and add the stock, fish sauce, carrots and potatoes. Bring to a simmer then cover and transfer to the oven. Cook for 2–2½ hours, or until the meat is tender. Add the coconut milk to the curry 30 minutes before the end of cooking. Serve immediately with the baguette. **SERVES 4**

SPICED STEAK FAJITAS WITH PINEAPPLE SALSA I adore Mexican food. By that, I don't mean stodgy refried beans, orange cheese and thick sour cream, but the real thing: a celebration of fresh lime, chilli and juicy just-seared meat.

250g fresh pineapple,
  cut into chunks
½ red chilli, sliced lengthways
  and finely chopped
½ green chilli, sliced lengthways
  and finely chopped
4 spring onions, finely chopped
3 tablespoons light-flavoured oil
juice 1 lime
3 tablespoons roughly
  chopped coriander
1 teaspoon dried chilli flakes
¼ teaspoon cayenne pepper
2 rump steaks (about 350g each)
1 red pepper, halved,
  deseeded and sliced
1 yellow pepper, halved,
  deseeded and sliced
1 red onion, halved and sliced
2 garlic cloves, crushed
1 teaspoon ground cumin
8 flour tortillas, warmed
2 limes, halved

To make the salsa, place the pineapple, red and green chilli, spring onion, 1 tablespoon of the oil, lime juice and coriander in a bowl and toss gently to combine. Cover and set aside until needed.

Combine the chilli flakes and cayenne in a small bowl and season well with sea salt and freshly ground black pepper. Rub the steaks with 1 tablespoon of the oil and sprinkle the spice mix on both sides. Place a griddle on medium heat and when hot add the steaks. Cook for 2 minutes on each side, or a minute or so longer if you prefer your steaks medium. Cover and leave to rest.

In a bowl toss together the peppers, onion, garlic, cumin and remaining tablespoon of oil. Cook on the griddle for 3–4 minutes, tossing occasionally, until slightly brown and tender.

To serve, slice the steaks and place a few strips on a tortilla. Top with the pepper and onion mixture, the salsa and a squeeze of lime juice. **SERVES 4**

'I can't look at this on the plate and not think
of margaritas. Make a jug to serve with your
spiced steak fajitas – even if it is a school night!'

GOULASH WITH GNOCCHI AND SOURED CREAM There are no short cuts here, but with this in the oven you have the perfect excuse to lie on the sofa and read the Sunday papers for three hours while you 'keep an eye on it'.

3 tablespoons plain flour
3 tablespoons paprika
1 teaspoon sea salt
1.5kg chuck or blade steak,
　cut into 5cm pieces
500g onions, sliced
3 garlic cloves, sliced
1 red chilli, finely chopped
2 tablespoons tomato purée
125ml red wine vinegar
500ml beef stock
400g tin chopped tomatoes
2 bay leaves
2 strips lemon peel
1 tablespoon olive oil
small knob unsalted butter
250g button mushrooms, sliced
handful flat-leaf parsley, chopped
500g gnocchi, cooked according
　to packet instructions
dollop soured cream
　sprinkled with paprika

Preheat the oven to 160°C/gas mark 3. Put the flour, 1 tablespoon of the paprika, salt and freshly ground black pepper in a bowl and stir to combine. Add the steak and toss to coat, shake off excess flour and place in a large casserole dish.

Add the onion, garlic, chilli, tomato purée, the remaining paprika, vinegar, stock, tomatoes, bay leaves and lemon peel. Bring to the boil over medium heat, then cover the dish and transfer to the oven. Cook for 3 hours.

To finish, heat the oil and butter in a frying pan over medium heat and cook the mushrooms for 3–5 minutes. Stir into the goulash and scatter with parsley. Serve with gnocchi and soured cream.
SERVES 4

Leg of lamb

Twenty years ago there was a genius advert on Australian television – a young Naomi Watts turned down a date with Tom Cruise because her mum was cooking lamb roast for dinner. It's one of our most famous and favourite ads of all time and neatly sums up my meat credentials: I'm an Aussie; I love lamb roast. When my dad was a butcher, he'd buy a whole sheep at market for $20. Now a good leg of lamb costs more than that and, when we're cooking it, we're damn well going to make sure it's something special.

LAMB WITH TORN BREAD AND APRICOT STUFFING + CARAMELISED CHICORY

You need decent bread for this stuffing – fortunately it's easy enough to find these days. (Better head back out to that farmers' market.)

60g unsalted butter
1 onion, chopped
1 garlic clove, crushed
2 teaspoons cumin seeds
200g sourdough bread,
   torn into bite-sized pieces
2 teaspoons dried chilli flakes
150g dried apricots,
   roughly chopped
50g pistachio nuts,
   roughly chopped
1 tablespoon olive oil, for brushing
2kg lamb leg, bone in

Heat the butter in a large frying pan over medium heat. Add the onion and cook, stirring occasionally, for 6–8 minutes until softened. Add the garlic and 1 teaspoon cumin seeds and cook for another minute. Tip the mixture into a large bowl and add the torn bread, chilli flakes, dried apricots and pistachio nuts and season well with sea salt and freshly ground black pepper. Set aside until needed.

Preheat the oven to 190°C/gas mark 5. Mix the olive oil with the remaining cumin seeds and brush over the entire surface of the lamb. Place the lamb in a large roasting tin and roast for 1 hour 20 minutes, or until cooked to your liking. About 15 minutes before the end of cooking place the stuffing mixture around the lamb. Cover loosely with foil and leave to rest for 15 minutes before carving. Serve with the caramelised chicory. **SERVES 4–6**

CARAMELISED CHICORY

4 chicory heads,
   halved lengthways
3 red onions, cut into wedges
3 tablespoons soft brown sugar
½ teaspoon dried chilli flakes
2 tablespoons olive oil
2 tablespoons cider vinegar

While the lamb is roasting, put the chicory and onions in a baking dish and sprinkle with the sugar and chilli flakes. Drizzle with the oil and vinegar and season to taste with sea salt and freshly ground black pepper. Place in the oven and cook for 35–45 minutes, until golden and caramelised. Serve hot.

CLASSIC LAMB STEW Anglo-Australians of my generation had to put up with old-fashioned Irish stew when we were children...no seasoning, no herbs, no flavour, no seconds required. This version is my attempt to wipe out that memory.

1.5kg boneless lamb leg,
  cut into 7cm chunks
2 medium onions,
  each cut into 8 wedges
3 medium carrots,
  cut into 5cm chunks
3 celery sticks,
  cut into 5cm chunks
250ml white wine
500ml lamb or beef stock
2 tablespoons tomato purée
4 tablespoons good
  balsamic vinegar
6 garlic cloves, finely sliced
2 long rosemary sprigs
2 bay leaves

Preheat the oven to 240°C/gas mark 8. Put the lamb, onions, carrots and celery in a large roasting tray and season well with sea salt and freshly ground black pepper. Roast for 20 minutes, turning once, until the lamb and vegetables are lightly browned. Reduce the oven temperature to 180°C/gas mark 4.

Remove the lamb and vegetables from the roasting tray and place in a large ovenproof dish with a lid. Add the wine, stock, tomato purée and vinegar. Scatter the garlic over the lamb and add the rosemary sprigs and bay leaves. Season with more salt and pepper and toss lightly. Place the lid on the dish and bake for 2 hours, or until the lamb is very tender. SERVES 6–8

HERB ROLLED LEG OF LAMB + MINT MASHED PEAS I've never quite fallen in love with battered cod and chips, but minted mushy peas are my new passion.

1.7kg rolled lamb leg
  (easy carve) or boneless
  joint, trimmed of excess fat
olive oil, for drizzling
4 garlic cloves, crushed
2 tablespoons chopped rosemary
  leaves, plus extra to serve
6 good-quality anchovies

Preheat the oven to 200°C/gas mark 6. Drizzle the lamb with olive oil and season with sea salt and freshly ground black pepper. Place the lamb in a roasting tray and roast for 1 hour.

Place the garlic, rosemary, anchovies and a pinch of sea salt in a mortar and pestle and pound to a rough paste. Remove the lamb from the oven, spread the paste over the surface of the lamb and cook for a further 20 minutes, or until the lamb is cooked to your liking. Transfer to a warm place to rest for 15 minutes, loosely covered with foil.

Sprinkle the lamb with extra rosemary and serve with the mint mashed peas. **SERVES 4–6**

MINT MASHED PEAS

1 tablespoon olive oil
1 onion, chopped
2 garlic cloves, crushed
125ml chicken stock
500g frozen peas
small handful mint leaves,
  roughly chopped

Heat the olive oil in a saucepan over medium heat. Add the onion and cook until just starting to colour. Add the garlic and cook for 2 minutes, or until slightly golden. Add the stock and peas and cook gently for 3 minutes, or until warmed through. Transfer to a food processor or blender and pulse 2–3 times until slightly broken up, or mash lightly in the pan. Add the mint leaves and season to taste.

SLOW ROASTED LAMB LEG + CHILLI RELISH For me, chilli relish is up there with the other wonders of the universe – how can something so simple be so delicious?

2kg lamb leg, with bone
1 whole head garlic,
    cut in half crossways
handful sage leaves
800g charlotte or new potatoes,
    cut into small chunks
3 tablespoons olive oil
2 rosemary sprigs
2 heads fennel, trimmed and
    finely sliced on a mandolin
handful flat-leaf parsley
2 tablespoons olive oil
2 tablespoons lemon juice

Preheat the oven to 160°C/gas mark 3. Season the lamb with sea salt and freshly ground black pepper and place in a baking dish with the garlic and sage. Add 250ml water and cover with foil. Roast for 3 hours, checking the lamb from time to time and adding more water as it evaporates. Continue adding water up to 2½ hours of cooking.

After 2 hours, place the potatoes in another baking dish with the olive oil and rosemary. Toss and season well and place in the oven.

After 3 hours, toss the potatoes and uncover the lamb. Increase the oven to 220°C/gas mark 7 and roast for a further 20–30 minutes, until brown. The meat should be tender and falling off the bone.

Place the fennel, parsley, olive oil, lemon juice and a pinch of sea salt in a bowl and gently toss to combine. Serve the lamb and potatoes with the fennel salad and the chilli relish. **SERVES 4–6**

CHILLI RELISH

6 long red chillies,
    deseeded and diced
2 tablespoons finely chopped
    flat-leaf parsley
1 garlic clove, crushed
125ml olive oil

Place the chilli, parsley and garlic in a bowl and stir to combine. Heat the oil in a small saucepan over medium–high heat. When hot, pour the oil over the chilli mixture. Set aside for a few minutes while the flavours develop then season to taste.

LAMB TAGINE WITH TOMATOES If you've ever been given a Moroccan tagine pot, now is the time to get it out of the cupboard and let it work its magic.

3 tablespoons olive oil
1kg lamb leg meat,
  cut into 5cm chunks
1 red onion, finely chopped
2 garlic cloves, crushed
1 tablespoon grated ginger
1 tablespoon ras el hanout
1 cinnamon stick
2 tablespoons soft brown sugar
1 tablespoon fish sauce
4 tomatoes, roughly chopped
1 teaspoon grated lime zest
500ml chicken stock
2 desiree potatoes
  (about 400g), chopped
2 sweet potatoes
  (about 500g), chopped
400g couscous, prepared
  to packet instructions
large handful coriander leaves,
  roughly chopped
handful roasted almonds,
  roughly chopped

Preheat the oven to 160°C/gas mark 3. Heat a tablespoon of the olive oil in a large frying pan over high heat. Add half the lamb and cook for 2 minutes each side, or until well browned. Remove and place in a tagine or a baking dish. Repeat this step with more oil and the remaining lamb.

Reduce heat to medium and place the remaining olive oil and the onion into the pan. Cook for 5 minutes, stirring occasionally, until the onion is translucent. Add the garlic and ginger and cook for 1 minute, then add the ras el hanout and cinnamon and cook for another minute, stirring. Add the sugar, fish sauce, tomatoes, lime zest and stock and bring to the boil. Remove from heat.

Add the potatoes and sweet potatoes to the tagine and pour the sauce over the top. Cover and bake for 2 hours, or until the lamb is tender.

Prepare the couscous according to the instructions on the packet and toss with some of the coriander. Serve the tagine in separate bowls, dressed with the coriander and almonds. **SERVES 4**

BARBECUED LAMB LEG WITH THYME AND HARISSA DRESSING At the risk of sounding like a smug cravat-wearing foodie, this dish always reminds me of the south of France. I ate it under an olive tree – I wasn't wearing a cravat, of course.

1.5kg boneless lamb leg
(not rolled)
100ml olive oil
2 teaspoons thyme leaves,
plus extra to serve
2 garlic cloves, crushed
2 tablespoons lemon juice
2 teaspoons harissa
500g mixed heirloom cherry
tomatoes, halved
¼ red onion, finely sliced
½ lemon, peeled, pith removed
and sliced into thin rounds
2 tablespoons extra-virgin
olive oil
1 tablespoon sherry vinegar

Trim excess fat off the lamb but leave the skin on. Combine 2 tablespoons olive oil, the thyme and garlic in a bowl. Rub the lamb with the oil mixture and season with sea salt and freshly ground black pepper. Preheat a gas barbecue to medium–high. Place the lamb skin side down and turn the burners off directly under the lamb but keep the side burners on medium heat. Close the lid and cook for 20 minutes, turning around after 10 minutes. Turn over and cook for a further 20 minutes, or until cooked to medium rare.

Meanwhile, to make the harissa dressing, place the remaining olive oil, lemon juice and harissa in a large heatproof dish. Once the lamb is cooked, place the hot lamb in the marinade and set aside to rest for 15 minutes, turning once to coat.

Arrange the tomatoes, onion and lemon slices on a serving plate. Lightly whisk the extra-virgin olive oil and vinegar, season well and then dress the salad.

Remove the lamb from the marinade and thinly slice. Serve drizzled with the harissa dressing and the salad. Sprinkle with the extra thyme. **SERVES 4–6**

Pork chop

When my mum wanted to serve up a 'fancy dinner' back in the seventies, she'd crack open a tin of pineapple rings and arrange them lovingly over a tray of pork chops. We've come a long way from the pineapple, but Mum's idea that pork should be paired up with something sweet was, of course, perfectly sound. When I came to write this chapter, I realised my favourite easy pork dishes all work along the same lines: pork teamed with sweet roasted red pepper in a romesco sauce, orange zest, apples caramelised in maple syrup and marsala. Thanks for the tip, Mum.

MANCHEGO CRUSTED PORK + ROMESCO SAUCE If you don't have manchego cheese in the fridge, parmesan will do the job just fine here.

120g toasted breadcrumbs
100g manchego cheese,
 finely grated
handful flat-leaf parsley,
 roughly chopped
zest 1 lemon
75g plain flour
1 egg
1 tablespoon milk
4 pork cutlets (about 270g each)
125ml olive oil
lemon wedges

Preheat the oven to 180°C/gas mark 4. Mix the breadcrumbs, manchego, parsley and lemon zest in a bowl and season with sea salt and freshly ground black pepper. Place the flour on a large plate and beat the egg and milk together in a separate bowl. Dip the cutlets into the flour and shake off any excess. Coat them with the egg and milk mixture and then dip both sides into the breadcrumbs, pressing the crumbs into the pork.

Heat the oil in a frying pan over medium–high heat and fry the cutlets for 4 minutes on each side, or until lightly golden. Place the cutlets on a wire rack over a roasting tray and roast for 10–15 minutes, or until cooked. Cover and leave to rest for 5 minutes before serving with the romesco sauce and lemon wedges.
SERVES 4

ROMESCO SAUCE

2 red peppers, deseeded
 and cut into chunks
½ head garlic
olive oil, to drizzle
40g blanched almonds,
 lightly dry-toasted
½ teaspoon dried chilli flakes
2 tablespoons sherry vinegar
2 tablespoons extra-virgin
 olive oil

Preheat the oven to 180°C/gas mark 4. Place the peppers and garlic in a roasting tin, drizzle with the oil and roast for 15–20 minutes. When cool enough to handle, squeeze the garlic into a blender, add the roasted peppers and all the other ingredients and pulse to combine, making sure the sauce still retains some texture.

ORANGE AND OREGANO MARINATED PORK The hardest question journalists ask me is, 'What's the next big food trend?' I don't think I've ever answered 'Cuban', so here's my Cuban pork. Remember, you heard it here first, folks...

3 garlic cloves, peeled
1 teaspoon cumin seeds
1 tablespoon roughly chopped
  oregano leaves
¼ teaspoon dried chilli flakes
finely grated zest and
  juice of ½ orange
½ teaspoon flaked sea salt
1 tablespoon lime juice
2 tablespoons olive oil
4 pork chops (about 200g each)
handful roughly chopped
  flat-leaf parsley
zest strips from
  remaining ½ orange
large handful salad leaves
balsamic vinegar, to drizzle

Use a mortar and pestle to pound the garlic, cumin seeds, oregano, chilli flakes, orange zest and salt into a thick aromatic paste. Transfer to a larger bowl and stir in the orange juice, lime juice and olive oil. Season with freshly ground black pepper. Add the chops and leave to marinate in the fridge for 15 minutes.

Preheat a barbecue or chargrill pan to medium–high. Drain the pork, reserving the marinade. Grill for 8–10 minutes, or until cooked through, turning once and brushing with the marinade halfway through.

Allow the pork to rest for 10 minutes. Sprinkle with parsley and the extra orange zest and serve with salad leaves drizzled with balsamic vinegar. **SERVES 4**

FENNEL ROASTED RACK OF PORK WITH MAPLE APPLES Butcher's pork will crisp up better than plastic-wrapped supermarket meat, but the trick of pouring boiling water over the skin and patting it dry will ensure perfect crackling.

1kg rack of pork (4 rib bones),
  skin scored
1 tablespoon olive oil
2 teaspoons sea salt
3 teaspoons fennel seeds,
  lightly toasted and crushed
1 garlic clove, crushed
4 tablespoons maple syrup
2 tablespoons lemon juice
3 apples, peeled and
  cut into 8 wedges
3 red onions, quartered

Preheat the oven to 230°C/gas mark 8. To ensure a crispy skin, pour 250ml boiling water over the pork skin and pat dry with kitchen paper. Place the rack in a roasting tray lined with baking paper. Drizzle with the oil and rub the salt and fennel seeds over the skin and into the scores. Roast for 30 minutes.

Meanwhile, combine the garlic, maple syrup and lemon juice in a large bowl and toss with the apples and onions. Season well with sea salt and freshly ground black pepper.

Reduce the oven heat to 180°C/gas mark 4. Remove the tray and scatter the apples and onions around the pork. Roast for a further 45 minutes, turning the apples and onions halfway through.

Remove the pork from the oven and transfer to a warm dish to rest for 10–15 minutes. If needed, leave the apples and onions to continue cooking, until they are tender and caramelised. Cut the pork into four portions, between the bones, and serve with the apples and onions. **SERVES 4**

STUFFED PORK CHOPS WITH MARSALA The prosciutto and sage stuffing and the syrupy marsala gravy give a definite nod to Italy here. *Buon appetito!*

4 pork cutlets (about 270g
   each), rind removed
4 large sage leaves
4 slices prosciutto
75g plain flour
2 tablespoons olive oil
2 tablespoons butter
125ml marsala
125ml chicken stock
250g baby spinach leaves

Preheat the oven to 180°C/gas mark 4. Carefully cut a long deep pocket through the fat on each cutlet and stuff with a sage leaf and a slice of prosciutto. Place the flour on a plate and season well with sea salt and freshly ground black pepper.

Heat the oil and butter in a large frying pan over medium–high heat. Lightly dredge the cutlets in the flour, place immediately in the hot pan and cook for 4–5 minutes on each side. Transfer to a roasting tray and roast for 10 minutes, until cooked.

Add the marsala to the frying pan and use a wooden spoon to scrape up any brown bits that have stuck to the bottom. Continue cooking until the quantity is reduced by a half, then add the chicken stock, lower the heat to medium and cook for 1 minute more, stirring, until the sauce thickens. Return the pork and any juices that have collected in the tray to the pan, turning over carefully to coat with sauce.

Place a large frying pan over a medium heat. Add the spinach and cook until just wilted. Drain off any excess water and season well. Serve immediately with the cutlets. **SERVES 4**

BRAISED PORK CHOPS WITH LEEK AND MUSTARD There's a hint of Alsace about this – serve with mashed potatoes and heavy rain lashing against the windows.

4 pork chops (about 270g each)
2 tablespoons olive oil
100g bacon, chopped
1 leek, sliced
2 garlic cloves, crushed
1 tablespoon roughly
   chopped thyme
2 tablespoons roughly
   chopped rosemary
300ml chicken stock
125ml soured cream
1–2 teaspoons Dijon mustard

Preheat the oven to 180°C/gas mark 4. Season the chops with sea salt and freshly ground black pepper. Heat the oil in a large casserole dish over medium heat and quickly brown the chops on both sides. Set aside.

Fry the bacon until lightly crisp then add the leek and cook until starting to soften. Add the garlic, thyme and half the rosemary, stir briefly and then return the chops to the dish. Pour over the chicken stock. Transfer the dish to the oven and cook, covered, for 20 minutes. Remove the lid and cook for a further 15–20 minutes, or until the pork is tender and cooked through. Remove the chops and set aside to rest.

Add the soured cream and mustard to the casserole dish and bring to the boil over low heat, stirring constantly. Garnish with the remaining rosemary and serve with the chops. **SERVES 4**

THAI STYLE MARINATED PORK + CHILLI DRESSING If you really can't be bothered making the dressing (and we all have those days), use sweet chilli sauce with a squeeze of fresh lime juice and chopped chilli to give it a boost.

4 brown shallots, sliced
1 tablespoon grated ginger
2 garlic cloves, crushed
handful coriander, including
    stems, coarsely chopped
2 teaspoons soy sauce
1 tablespoon fish sauce
1 tablespoon caster sugar
4 pork cutlets (about 200g each)
small handful mint leaves
½ long cucumber,
    roughly chopped

CHILLI DRESSING

2 tablespoons rice wine vinegar
1½ tablespoons caster sugar
1 tablespoon fish sauce
1 long red chilli, finely chopped
1 tablespoon finely sliced
    spring onion
½ long cucumber, deseeded
    and finely diced

Put the shallots, ginger, garlic, coriander, soy sauce, fish sauce, sugar, sea salt and freshly ground black pepper in a food processor and process to a paste. Transfer to a shallow non-metallic dish and add the cutlets. Mix well then cover and leave to marinate in the fridge for a minimum 15 minutes.

Preheat a barbecue or chargrill pan to medium–high heat and brush lightly with oil. Grill the cutlets for 3–4 minutes on each side, or until cooked to your liking. Serve with the chilli dressing, mint leaves and cucumber. **SERVES 4**

Place the vinegar, sugar and fish sauce in a bowl and stir until the sugar has dissolved. Stir in the chilli, spring onion and cucumber. Set aside.

MERGUEZ SAUSAGES WITH LENTILS AND CAVOLO NERO In Italy, sausages with lentils is a traditional New Year's Day dinner. The lentils represent coins and good fortune. (I'm not sure about the sausages and cabbage!)

250g Puy lentils
1 red onion, finely chopped
2 garlic cloves, crushed
250ml chicken stock
250ml water
1 tablespoon olive oil
450g merguez sausages
250g cavolo nero, thinly sliced

Rinse the lentils under cold running water and drain well. Place them in a saucepan with the onion, garlic, stock and water. Bring to the boil then reduce heat and simmer for 25 minutes, or until the lentils are tender and the liquid is absorbed. Remove from the heat and season to taste with sea salt and freshly ground black pepper.

Heat the oil in a large frying pan over medium–high heat and cook the sausages for 5–6 minutes, or until browned and cooked through. Remove from the pan. Add the cavolo nero to the pan and cook until it is just starting to wilt. Serve with the lentils and sausages.

SERVES 4

CEVAPCICI WITH RADICCHIO AND LEMON Making your own sausages might seem frankly crazy in these hurried times, but these little ones are delicious and very easy. Roll up your sleeves and bask in the warm glow of achievement.

300g beef mince
300g lamb mince
2 tablespoons finely chopped
   flat-leaf parsley
2 teaspoons sea salt
2 garlic cloves, minced
¼ teaspoon cayenne pepper
1 teaspoon paprika
½ small onion, finely chopped
leaves from 1 small radicchio,
   roughly torn
extra-virgin olive oil, to drizzle
lemon wedges

Place the mince, parsley, salt, garlic, cayenne pepper, paprika and onion in a bowl and mix well. Leave to infuse for 15 minutes at room temperature. Form the mixture into 20 little sausages.

Heat a barbecue or chargrill pan to medium–high heat. Grill the cevapcici for 10–12 minutes, turning minimally but cooking all sides, until brown and cooked through. Serve immediately with radicchio drizzled with olive oil, lemon wedges and sea salt.

MAKES 20

CHILLI, SAUSAGE AND BROCCOLI PIZZA Being the swot that I am, when I'm making pizza dough I roll out extra bases and freeze them for emergency dinners.

polenta, for dusting
1 quantity basic pizza dough,
  or 4 pre-made pizza bases
375g buffalo mozzarella, torn
1 bunch tenderstem broccoli,
  halved lengthways and
  crossways
4 good-quality rustic pork
  sausages, squeezed out
  of skins in pieces
4 pinches dried chilli flakes
extra-virgin olive oil, to drizzle

Preheat the oven to 250°C/gas mark 9 and dust four 30cm pizza trays or two large oven trays with the polenta.

Dust the work surface lightly with flour. Turn the pizza dough out and knead for 1 minute to knock back, then divide into 4 pieces. Cover with oiled cling film and leave to rest for 15 minutes.

Flatten out one piece of dough into a rough circle with the palm of your hand. Gently roll out to a 30cm circle and transfer to a pizza or oven tray.

Add a quarter of the toppings to each pizza as you make them: buffalo mozzarella, broccoli, sausage pieces, pinch of chilli flakes and a drizzle of olive oil. Bake each pizza, one at a time, for 6–10 minutes, or until the base is coloured and crisp. **MAKES 4 PIZZAS**

BASIC PIZZA DOUGH

2 teaspoons dried instant yeast
1 tablespoon olive oil
½ tablespoon honey
375g strong white bread flour
1 teaspoon sea salt

Pour 250–300ml tepid water into a small bowl, sprinkle in the yeast, olive oil and honey and whisk with a fork until dissolved. Set aside.

By hand: Mix the flour and salt together in a large bowl. Make a well in the centre and pour in the yeast mixture. Bring together to form a soft dough, then turn out and knead well for 10 minutes until smooth and elastic.

By mixer: Put the flour and salt into an electric mixer fitted with a dough hook. With the mixer on slow speed, pour in most of the yeast liquid. Add the remaining liquid (plus a dash extra water if needed) until you have a soft dough. Continue kneading for 10–15 minutes, scraping the dough off the hook every so often if it becomes stuck. When the dough is smooth and elastic, turn onto a lightly floured surface and knead by hand for 1 minute to form a smooth ball.

Place the dough in a lightly greased large bowl and brush the top with a little olive oil. Cover with oiled cling film and leave the dough to rise in a warm place for 45 minutes or until doubled in size.

GINGER PORK FRIED RICE WITH EGG PANCAKE As far as I'm concerned, you can't be too gingery or garlicky. That's only if you're pork mince, of course.

3 tablespoons light-flavoured oil,
  plus extra for pancakes
3cm piece ginger, julienned
2 garlic cloves, chopped
500g pork mince
1 leek, white part only,
  halved and sliced
6 spring onions, finely sliced,
  plus extra spring onions, cut
  into 2cm lengths, to serve
3 long green chillies,
  finely chopped
650g cooked long-grain
  white rice (see page 35)
handful fried shallots
  (shop bought), optional
4 large eggs, beaten
sesame oil, to drizzle

Place a wok over medium heat. Add 2 tablespoons of the oil and stir-fry the ginger and garlic until starting to colour. Increase heat to high, add the mince and cook until well browned. Set aside. Add the remaining oil then the leek, sliced spring onion and chilli, and cook, stirring, for 2–3 minutes, or until softened. Add the rice and stir until warmed through. Return the mince to the wok and season to taste with sea salt and freshly ground black pepper. Transfer to a serving plate and sprinkle with the fried shallots.

Heat a large non-stick frying pan over medium heat. Lightly wipe with oil and pour in a small amount of egg to make a very thin pancake. Pour off any excess egg. Cook for 1 minute, or until lightly golden, then turn over and cook the other side for a further minute. Remove and keep warm whilst you cook the remaining egg. Tightly roll the pancakes and cut into ribbons. Serve with the fried rice, the extra spring onions and a drizzle of sesame oil. **SERVES 4**

ROASTED SAUSAGES WITH PEPPERS AND ONIONS I like sausage filling coarsely chopped in the Italian style. It seems most of England outvotes me on that.

8 coarse Italian sausages
2 yellow peppers,
  sliced lengthways
2 red peppers,
  sliced engthways
1 red onion, cut into thin wedges
½ teaspoon dried chilli flakes
1 teaspoon fennel seeds
1 tablespoon balsamic vinegar
large handful basil leaves
crusty bread rolls

Preheat the oven to 200°C/gas mark 6. Place the sausages, peppers and onion wedges in a baking dish and scatter over the chilli flakes, fennel seeds, sea salt and freshly ground black pepper. Roast in the oven for 45 minutes or until well browned.

Drizzle with balsamic and serve with fresh basil leaves and crusty bread rolls. **SERVES 4**

LAMB KOFTA MEATBALLS IN CURRY SAUCE When India meets Italy, great things result. Fry these meatballs in a pan, or toss them in oil on a tray and bake instead.

500g lamb mince
1 onion, coarsely grated
2 garlic cloves, crushed
25g fresh white breadcrumbs
finely grated zest 1 lemon
3 tablespoons chopped coriander
3 tablespoons chopped mint,
 plus extra handful, to serve
3 tablespoons light-flavoured oil
4 tablespoons korma curry paste
1 tablespoon finely chopped ginger
400g tin chopped tomatoes
200ml coconut milk
1 cinnamon stick
1 red onion, finely sliced
naan bread, warmed

Place the mince, onion, garlic, breadcrumbs, lemon zest, coriander and 3 tablespoons mint in a large mixing bowl. Add plenty of sea salt and freshly ground black pepper and combine thoroughly. Rinse your hands under cold water and, without drying, shape the mixture into 24 small meatballs.

Place a large non-stick frying pan over medium–high heat. Add 1 tablespoon of the oil and, when hot, add half the meatballs and fry for 4–5 minutes, turning often, until lightly browned on all sides. Transfer to a plate and repeat with more oil and remaining kofta.

Return the pan to the heat, add the remaining oil, curry paste and ginger. Fry for 1 minute, stirring constantly. Tip the tomatoes and coconut milk into the pan and stir well. Add the cinnamon stick and season with a little sea salt and plenty of black pepper. Bring to the boil then reduce the heat and simmer gently for 3 minutes.

Return the kofta to the pan and cook in the curry sauce for a further 5 minutes, until tender and cooked through. Serve scattered with the red onion slices, mint leaves and naan bread. **SERVES 4**

Pack of pasta

What on earth would we do without pasta in the cupboard? It's difficult to grasp that we non-Italians have been enjoying pasta for only one or two generations; already it's impossible to imagine our kitchens without it. How would we feed our children? I reach for the pasta pack several times a week; it's so easy that sometimes I feel guilty, as if I'm not making a 'proper' meal. Then I get over myself. This miracle energy source can be cooked up with just about any vegetable in the fridge, any tin in the cupboard, any meat or fish, to make a fantastic healthy meal that I know will be loved to the last mouthful. That's a real big 'easy'.

PORK RAGU WITH HERB PANGRATTATO In Italy, *pangrattato* breadcrumbs get called the 'poor man's parmesan'. I suppose breadcrumbs are cheaper than cheese. There's nothing 'poor man' here – the sourdough crumbs add fantastic crunch.

5 tablespoons olive oil
1kg boneless pork loin
1 onion, chopped
3 tablespoons roughly chopped
   rosemary leaves
6 garlic cloves, crushed
2 strips lemon peel
1 bay leaf
400g tin chopped tomatoes
250ml chicken stock
400g dried pappardelle
100g sourdough bread,
   pulsed until coarse crumbs
finely grated zest 1 lemon
3 tablespoons finely chopped
   flat-leaf parsley, plus extra,
   to serve

Preheat the oven to 160°C/gas mark 3. Heat 3 tablespoons olive oil in a heavy casserole dish over medium–high heat (the pork needs to be a tight fit in the dish). Season the pork well with sea salt and freshly ground black papper and sear on all sides until golden brown. Remove the pork and set aside.

Add the onion to the dish and cook for 5 minutes, or until softened. Add 2 tablespoons rosemary and 4 garlic cloves and cook for a further 2 minutes. Add the lemon peel, bay leaf, tomatoes and stock. Return the pork to the dish, bring to a simmer and transfer to the oven. Cook for 2½–3 hours or until the pork is meltingly tender. Remove from the dish and when cool enough to handle, shred into small pieces, discarding any fat. Return the meat to the dish, season and reheat.

Cook the pappardelle in a large saucepan of salted water for 2 minutes less than the instructions on the packet, or until al dente.

Place a large frying pan over medium heat, add the remaining olive oil and garlic, breadcrumbs and lemon zest and cook, tossing regularly, until golden. Let cool slightly, then add the remaining rosemary and 3 tablespoons parsley and season well.

Gently toss the ragù with the pappardelle. Sprinkle with the pangrattato and extra parsley. **SERVES 4**

PASTA PUTTANESCA While this dish might be an Italian classic, it's also the perfect throw-together of whatever you happen to have in the fridge — those *puttane* certainly knew how to use their leftovers.

60ml olive oil
2 large garlic cloves, sliced
½ teaspoon dried chilli flakes
3 good-quality anchovies,
  chopped
100g pitted green olives,
  roughly chopped
300g cherry tomatoes, halved
2 tablespoons capers
400g dried penne, cooked
  to packet instructions
large handful shredded basil
parmesan cheese, shaved

Heat the oil in a frying pan over medium heat. Add the garlic, chilli flakes and anchovies and cook for a few minutes. Add the olives, tomatoes and capers and cook for a few more minutes, until the tomatoes have softened and everything has heated through.

Stir into the pasta and serve dressed with the basil, parmesan and freshly ground black pepper. **SERVES 4**

COURGETTE AND TUNA SPAGHETTI This is a quick weekday dinner that can be on the table 10 minutes after you've got home from ferrying children to all those vitally important activities they can't miss out on.

300g dried spaghetti
2 tablespoons olive oil
3 medium courgettes,
  peeled into ribbons
2 garlic cloves, crushed
zest and juice 1 lemon
handful flat-leaf parsley,
  roughly chopped, plus extra
  whole leaves, to serve
handful chives, roughly chopped
handful basil, roughly torn
160g tin tuna, drained and
  flaked into large chunks

Cook the spaghetti in a large saucepan of salted water, or according to the instructions on the packet, until al dente. Drain and refresh.

Place a large frying pan over high heat and drizzle with a little of the olive oil. Cook the courgette for 2–3 minutes, or until golden and softened, then remove and set aside. Reduce the heat to medium, add the remaining oil to the pan and cook the garlic for 1 minute, then add the lemon zest. Return the courgette to the pan with the parsley, chives, basil, tuna and spaghetti and toss gently to combine. Season with lemon juice and freshly ground black pepper and sprinkle with parsley to serve. **SERVES 4**

TALEGGIO AND PANCETTA BAKED PASTA OK, I admit it, this is really macaroni cheese – a nostalgic personal favourite that I try to slip into every book in a different cunning disguise. Nothing beats that combination of cheese and pasta.

300g dried rigatoni
2 teaspoons light-flavoured oil
200g pancetta, cubed
1 small onion, finely chopped
50g butter, plus extra
    for greasing
50g plain flour
580ml milk
250g taleggio cheese,
    rind removed
1½ tablespoons roughly
    chopped thyme

Preheat the oven to 210°C/gas mark 6. Cook the rigatoni in a large saucepan of boiling water for 8–10 minutes, or according to the instructions on the packet, until al dente. Drain and refresh.

While the pasta is cooking, place a large non-stick frying pan over medium–high heat. Add the oil and fry the pancetta for 4–5 minutes, stirring often, or until browned. Add the onion and cook for a further 5–6 minutes, stirring often, until softened.

Drop the butter into the pan and, when melted, stir in the flour and cook for 30 seconds. Gradually stir in the milk and bring to a gentle simmer. Cook for 5 minutes, stirring, or until thickened.

Cut the cheese into small cubes and stir two-thirds into the sauce. As soon as the cheese has melted, remove the pan from the heat, add 1 tablespoon thyme leaves and season to taste with sea salt and freshly ground black pepper.

Add the cooked rigatoni to the cheese sauce and combine well. Transfer to a lightly buttered ovenproof dish and dot the remaining cheese on top. Bake for 20–25 minutes, or until golden brown and bubbling. Sprinkle with the remaining thyme to serve. **SERVES 4**

ORZO, FETA AND ROASTED PEPPER SALAD Serve this with barbecued meat and a big leafy salad. There – that's all your summer entertaining sorted.

2 yellow peppers
2 red peppers
500g dried orzo
1 long red chilli, finely diced
1 garlic clove, crushed
1 teaspoon paprika
zest and juice of 1 lemon
4 tablespoons olive oil
large handful flat-leaf parsley
200g feta cheese, crumbled

Preheat the oven to 220°C/gas mark 7. Place the peppers on an oven tray lined with baking paper and roast for 30–35 minutes (the yellow peppers will cook more quickly), turning halfway through, until dark and blistered. Place in a bowl and cover immediately with cling film so the peppers will steam.

While the peppers are steaming, cook the orzo in a large pan of salted water, according to the instructions on the packet, until al dente. Drain and refresh. Meanwhile, place the chilli, garlic, paprika, lemon zest and olive oil in a small saucepan over medium heat and cook for 2 minutes, until warmed through. Remove the pan from the heat, add the lemon juice and season with sea salt and freshly ground black pepper.

Slip the skins off the peppers, remove their core and seeds and tear into strips. Place the cooked orzo, warmed dressing, peppers, parsley and feta in a large bowl and toss gently to combine. **SERVES 4**

SPICY PASTA AND SAUSAGE SOUP This soup could be described as 'rib-sticking' – it's the sort of hearty fare you eat on your knee in front of Sunday night telly.

3 tablespoons olive oil
500g good-quality spicy Italian
 sausages, meat squeezed
 from casings into pieces
2 large leeks, trimmed,
 halved and thinly sliced
1 fennel, chopped
2 teaspoons thyme leaves
2 garlic cloves, crushed
1 teaspoon dried chilli flakes
1 teaspoon fennel seeds, lightly
 toasted and roughly crushed
4 vine-ripened tomatoes, diced
1.5 litres chicken stock
250g small orecchiette
400g tin cannellini beans,
 rinsed and drained
handful flat-leaf parsley,
 roughly chopped

Heat half the oil in a large frying pan over high heat. Add the sausage pieces and cook for 3–4 minutes, until golden. Remove and drain on kitchen paper.

Reduce the heat to medium–low, add the remaining oil to the pan and cook the leek and fennel, stirring occasionally, for 6–7 minutes, or until softened. Add the thyme, garlic, chilli flakes and fennel seeds and cook, stirring, for 1–2 minutes or until fragrant. Add the tomato and cook for another minute.

Add the stock and bring to the boil. Add the orecchiette then reduce the heat and simmer, stirring occasionally, for 20 minutes, or until the pasta is just tender. Return the sausage to the pan with the cannellini beans, and cook for a further minute. Season to taste with sea salt and freshly ground black pepper. Serve sprinkled with parsley. **SERVES 4**

'When I'm making soup, my daughter Inès will always pour in a cupful of pasta while my back is turned. It's a great way to use up all those packs in the cupboard that have a little bit left in the bottom.'

Bag of rice

I'm always amazed by the enormous sacks of rice you see in Asian markets. I'm not a loyal cook – I like rice so much that I usually have about five varieties in my cupboard at any one time – so I can't imagine having just one big bag and not being allowed to use any other variety until I've eaten my way through it. There's a different rice for almost every culture and style of cooking, and although I'm not a stickler about many things, I am about this. I could no more eat basmati rice with Thai food, put brown rice in a risotto or use arborio for a stir-fry, than I could add banana to beef stew.

LEBANESE RICE AND LENTILS This is Middle Eastern comfort food. Enjoy on its own with the yoghurt, or serve with chicken roasted in lots of lemon and garlic.

3 tablespoons olive oil
2 onions, halved and sliced
3 garlic cloves, crushed
1 teaspoon ground cumin
1 teaspoon ground cinnamon
200g dried Puy lentils
100g long-grain white rice
800ml vegetable stock
dollop plain yoghurt mixed with
    ground cinnamon and cumin
2 tomatoes, quartered
handful mint and flat-leaf parsley
    leaves, roughly chopped

Heat the oil in a large saucepan over medium heat. Add the onion and cook for 10 minutes, or until soft and golden. Add the garlic, cumin and cinnamon and cook for 1–2 minutes, or until fragrant.

Add the lentils and rice and cook, stirring, for a further 2 minutes, then pour in the stock. Bring to the boil then reduce the heat and simmer for 25–30 minutes, until all the liquid is absorbed and the rice and lentils are tender. Season to taste with sea salt and freshly ground black pepper.

Serve the rice and lentils with the yoghurt, tomato chunks and mint and parsley leaves. **SERVES 4**

STIR-FRIED CURRY BROWN RICE WITH CASHEWS Brown rice has lots of flavour but it takes longer to cook, so double the quantity and enjoy it two nights running.

200g brown rice
3 tablespoons light-flavoured oil
2 teaspoons curry powder
6 spring onions, cut into
    4cm-long batons
2 heads pak choy, trimmed
    and quartered lengthways
200g mangetout, cut into strips
1 red chilli, halved
    and finely chopped
3 large eggs, beaten
3 tablespoons soy sauce
handful coriander leaves
100g roasted cashews, chopped

Cook the rice according to the instructions on the packet. Drain and refresh. Set aside until needed.

Heat 2 tablespoons of the oil in a wok over medium heat. Add the curry powder and stir-fry for 1 minute. Add the spring onion, pak choy, mangetout and chilli and fry for 2–4 minutes, until the vegetables are tender. Remove from the wok. Add the remaining oil to the wok and when hot add the eggs and scramble them until they are dry and golden brown.

Add the cooked rice and soy sauce and stir-fry for 2 minutes, until mixed together. Return the vegetables to the wok and stir through the cashews and coriander. Serve immediately. **SERVES 4**

'I used to work with a chef who would flake the meat from the smoked trout and then leave the trout heads lined up on the coffee machine to frighten the barista in the morning. Childish fun but fabulous!'

RICE SALAD WITH BROAD BEANS, ASPARAGUS AND SMOKED TROUT You can make this with fresh podded broad beans, frozen broad beans or just a bag of frozen peas. (That's called moving down a sliding scale from foodie to realist.)

500g basmati rice
500g frozen broad beans, blanched and refreshed (shelling optional)
300g asparagus, woody stems removed, sliced into little discs
2 tablespoons lemon juice
80ml extra-virgin olive oil
3 tablespoons finely chopped flat-leaf parsley
2 tablespoons finely chopped mint, plus extra whole leaves
4 spring onions, finely chopped, reserving some for garnish
300g hot smoked trout

Place the rice in a large saucepan of lightly salted water and bring to the boil over high heat. Reduce heat to medium and simmer for 10 minutes. Add the broad beans and asparagus and cook for 1–2 minutes until the vegetables are just cooked. Drain and spread evenly on a baking tray to cool.

Transfer to a serving dish, drizzle with the lemon juice and olive oil and season with sea salt and freshly ground black pepper. Add the parsley, mint and spring onion and toss gently to combine. Flake over the smoked trout and top with a few extra mint leaves and spring onion. Chill until ready to serve. **SERVES 4**

CHORIZO, CUMIN AND TOMATO RICE This is my hybrid child born of two favourite dishes: *arroz rojo* – the tomato rice that's served with just about every meal in Mexico – and Cajun 'dirty rice' from America's southern states.

1 tablespoon olive oil
2 garlic cloves, crushed
1 teaspoon ground cumin
1 teaspoon paprika
1 teaspoon ground coriander
300g basmati rice
400g tin chopped tomatoes
750ml–1 litre chicken stock
200g green beans
300g chorizo, chopped
200g chargrilled red pepper in olive oil, drained and sliced
handful coriander leaves

Heat the oil in a large frying pan over medium–high heat. Add the garlic and spices and cook for 1–2 minutes, until fragrant. Stir in the rice and mix well, then pour in the tomatoes and 750ml of the stock. Bring to the boil then cover the pan and reduce heat to a simmer. Cook for about 30 minutes until all the stock has been absorbed and the rice is cooked (you may need to add more stock throughout the cooking). Add the beans 5 minutes before the end of the cooking time. Season with sea salt and freshly ground black pepper and keep warm.

Heat a frying pan over medium–high heat and cook the chorizo for 5 minutes, or until golden brown. To serve, transfer the rice to a platter and top with the chorizo, sliced peppers and coriander leaves. Drizzle the oil from the chorizo pan over the top. **SERVES 4**

BAKED LEEK AND GOAT'S CHEESE RISOTTO + APPLE AND CELERY SALAD | I was always taught that you had to stand over the risotto pan and stir religiously for half an hour. I love rule-breaking, so I adore the controversial 'no-stir' risotto.

2 tablespoons olive oil
25g unsalted butter
1 medium onion, finely chopped
3 leeks, cut lengthways
    and finely sliced
2 garlic cloves, crushed
1 teaspoon sea salt
2 teaspoons chopped rosemary
    leaves, plus extra to serve
250g arborio rice
850ml chicken stock, heated
120g soft goat's cheese,
    rind removed and chopped
50g freshly grated
    parmesan cheese

APPLE AND CELERY SALAD

100g rocket leaves
1 celery stick, sliced lengthways
    and cut into batons
1 head yellow chicory, leaves torn
1 head purple chicory, leaves torn
1 red apple, cored
    and cut into thin wedges
handful walnuts, roughly chopped
1 tablespoon lemon juice
2 tablespoons extra-virgin
    olive oil

Preheat the oven to 200°C/gas mark 6. Heat a large ovenproof dish over medium heat. Add the olive oil, butter, onion, leek, garlic and sea salt, and cook, stirring occasionally, for 5–6 minutes, or until the vegetables are softened. Add the rosemary and rice and stir over the heat for another minute.

Pour in the stock and bring to the boil. Remove from the heat and stir in the cheeses. Cover and bake for 25–30 minutes, or until the rice is cooked al dente. Remove the cover and place under a hot grill for 5 minutes, or until the top is golden. Sprinkle with rosemary and serve with the apple and celery salad.
SERVES 4

Place the rocket, celery batons, chicory, apple and walnuts in a bowl and toss to combine. Dress with the lemon juice and olive oil and season well with freshly ground black pepper.

PEA AND FENNEL RISOTTO And, for anyone who doesn't enjoy rule-breaking and would rather eat their own wooden spoon than bake risotto, here's a traditional 'add-a-ladleful-of-stock-and-stir' version. Read a good book with your spare hand.

25g unsalted butter,
  plus a knob extra
1 tablespoon olive oil
1 medium onion, diced
1 fennel bulb, diced
  and fronds reserved
500g arborio rice
125ml white wine
1.25 litres chicken stock, heated
400g peas (fresh or frozen)
50g freshly grated
  parmesan cheese

Heat the butter and oil in a large heavy-based pan over medium heat. When the butter has melted, add the onion and fennel with a good pinch of sea salt and cook for 4–5 minutes, until soft.

Add the rice and mix well to coat. When the rice has become translucent, add the white wine and continue stirring until it has all been absorbed.

Start adding the hot stock one ladle at a time, stirring continuously, and not adding the next ladle until the previous one has been absorbed. After about 20–25 minutes, add the peas and keep cooking, adding more stock as necessary, until the rice is cooked and the texture is nicely creamy. Season with sea salt and freshly ground black pepper and stir through the parmesan and extra knob of butter. Cover and let it sit for a few minutes. Transfer to serving plates and scatter over the fennel fronds and more black pepper. **SERVES 4**

Handful of grains

After 2000 years in the wilderness, grains are making a massive comeback. Couscous was first to reappear on the scene; in the nineties it was everywhere, but don't hold that against it. Spelt is now the supermodel of the grain world, having her photo shot for every top magazine, even though she's more than two millennia old. Browsing through the worthy sacks of grains in the health food store always brings out the hippy in me, and Natalie loves to use quinoa with flaked tuna and fennel as a quick-fix, goodness-packed Saturday lunch, especially if she suspects we've missed out on a serving of vegetables during the week.

COUSCOUS WITH FETA AND CUMIN The brilliance of couscous is its speed. Just boil the water and you're there – that's classified as instantaneous in my kitchen.

3 tablespoons lemon juice
4 tablespoons extra-virgin
 olive oil
1 teaspoon ground cumin
1 teaspoon paprika
1 red chilli, finely chopped
250g couscous
300g carrots, quartered
 lengthways and sliced
2 tablespoons roughly chopped
 flat-leaf parsley
2 tablespoons roughly chopped
 coriander leaves
200g feta cheese, sliced
1 small red onion,
 halved and finely sliced
70g toasted pine nuts
2 teaspoons sumac

In a small bowl combine the lemon juice, olive oil, cumin, paprika and chilli. Season with sea salt and freshly ground black pepper and mix well.

Prepare the couscous according to the instructions on the packet. Cook the carrots in boiling water for 1–2 minutes, until tender. Drain and transfer to a large bowl with the couscous. Pour over the dressing, add the parsley and coriander and toss well.

Place on a serving platter and scatter with the sliced feta, onion, pine nuts and sumac. **SERVES 4**

SPELT, TOMATO, BASIL AND PECORINO SALAD Fresh and lovely, spelt is probably my favourite grain. I like this salad best with a young, mild pecorino.

250g spelt
80ml extra-virgin olive oil
1 tablespoon red wine vinegar
large handful basil leaves,
 roughly torn
large handful flat-leaf parsley
 leaves, roughly chopped
375g cherry tomatoes, halved
1 long cucumber, quartered
 lengthways and diced
250g young pecorino cheese,
 cubed

Place 1 litre water in a saucepan and bring to the boil over high heat. Add the spelt and simmer for 30–35 minutes, or until just tender. Drain and spread evenly on a tray to cool.

When cool, transfer to a large serving bowl, drizzle with the olive oil and vinegar, add the basil and parsley and season with sea salt and freshly ground black pepper. Stir gently to combine. Top with the cherry tomatoes, cucumber and pecorino and chill until ready to serve. **SERVES 4**

VEGETABLE AND SPELT SOUP + PISTOU If you want to be reckless and mix your grains, throw in some short, tube pasta like cannolicchi for the last 10 minutes of the cooking time. Another variation would be to use a jar of pesto for the pistou.

3 tablespoons olive oil
1 medium onion, finely chopped
1 celery stick, finely chopped
2 leeks, white part only,
    halved and sliced
3 garlic cloves, crushed
1 medium potato, diced
2 carrots, cubed
2 large courgettes,
    halved and chopped
200g green beans,
    halved lengthways
2 fresh bay leaves
2 tablespoons roughly chopped
    flat-leaf parsley
75g spelt, rinsed
1.5 litres vegetable stock, heated

Heat the oil in a large saucepan over medium heat. Add the onion, celery and leek and cook for 5 minutes, or until soft. Add the garlic and cook for 1–2 minutes. Add the potato, carrot, courgette, beans, bay leaves, parsley and spelt.

Cover with the stock and simmer for 35–40 minutes, or until the spelt is tender (if the soup is too thick add a little more stock). Season to taste with sea salt and freshly ground black pepper. Serve in individual bowls topped with a spoonful of the pistou. **SERVES 4–6**

PISTOU

5 garlic cloves
small handful basil leaves
60g parmesan cheese, crumbled
60ml extra-virgin olive oil

Place the garlic, basil and a pinch of sea salt in a mortar and pestle and pound until puréed. Add the parmesan and oil and mix together to make a paste.

ROASTED APRICOT YELLOW COUSCOUS WITH GRILLED FISH This is a plate of pure gold: golden grain, spices, apricots and fish. (Feel free to spoil the colour scheme with a bowl of thick garlicky yoghurt, if you like.)

250g couscous
310ml chicken stock
2 pinches saffron threads,
  crumbled
25g unsalted butter
8 apricots, halved and stoned
1 tablespoon light brown sugar
¼ teaspoon ground cumin
4 spring onions, sliced
3 tablespoons shelled pistachios,
  roughly chopped
4 firm white fish fillets,
  skin on (about 200g each)
2 tablespoons olive oil
handful coriander leaves
2 limes, halved

Place the couscous in a heatproof bowl. Combine the chicken stock, a pinch of sea salt and the saffron in a saucepan over medium–high heat and bring to the boil. Take off the heat, add the butter and stir until melted. Pour over the couscous, cover with cling film and set aside for 10 minutes.

Preheat the grill to high. Place the apricots cut-side up in a heatproof dish and sprinkle with the sugar, cumin, sea salt and freshly ground black pepper. Grill until bubbly and golden. Fluff up the couscous with a fork, then stir through the spring onion and apricots. Transfer to a serving bowl, season to taste and sprinkle with the pistachios.

Heat a frying pan over medium–high heat. Brush the fish with the olive oil and season well. Cook skin-side down for 3 minutes. Turn over and cook for 1 minute, until golden and just cooked through. Dress the fish with coriander and a squeeze of lime juice and serve with the apricot couscous. **SERVES 4**

QUINOA, TUNA AND FENNEL SALAD Here it is: our penance for the week. Just bursting with vegetables and protein, this will wipe away any traces of beer or pizza that have been consumed in the last few days and leave your body a temple.

150g quinoa
150g green beans, trimmed
   and cut into 3cm lengths
1 fennel bulb, finely sliced
425g tin tuna,
   drained and flaked
90g pitted green olives,
   thinly sliced
4 spring onions, thinly sliced
1 tablespoon lemon juice
2 tablespoons extra-virgin olive
   oil, plus extra to drizzle
handful tarragon and/or
   chervil leaves, roughly chopped

Rinse the quinoa well and place in a large saucepan with 500ml water. Bring to the boil then reduce heat to low. Cover and simmer for 12–15 minutes, until all the water has evaporated. Set aside to cool.

Blanch the beans in boiling water for 2 minutes then refresh in cold water. Place in a large bowl with the fennel, tuna and olives and toss to combine.

Place the quinoa in a bowl and stir in the spring onion, lemon juice and olive oil. Pile onto a serving platter and top with the vegetables and tuna. Drizzle over a little extra oil and sprinkle with herbs. **SERVES 4**

QUINOA FRITTERS When you're making the quinoa and tuna salad, cook up extra quinoa and make these the next day as a slightly less virtuous main course. This is another of those dishes that will make vegetarians fall at your feet with gratitude.

200g quinoa
2 large eggs, plus
   1 egg yolk, beaten
2 tablespoons roughly chopped
   flat-leaf parsley
2 tablespoons roughly chopped
   mint leaves
2 spring onions, finely chopped
60g feta cheese, crumbled
3 garlic cloves, crushed
1 teaspoon ground cumin
finely grated zest 1 lemon
4 tablespoons flour
2 tablespoons light-flavoured oil
thick Greek yoghurt
round lettuce leaves
2 limes, halved

Place the quinoa and 375ml water in a small saucepan. Cover and bring to the boil over high heat. Reduce heat to low and simmer gently for 12 minutes, or until the water has been absorbed and the quinoa is tender. When cool, measure out 2½ cups quinoa.

Combine the quinoa, beaten egg and a pinch of sea salt in a medium bowl. Stir in the parsley, mint, spring onion, feta, garlic, cumin and lemon zest. Add the flour and stir to combine. Form into 12 patties using a heaped tablespoon of the mixture for each one.

Heat the oil in a large frying pan over medium–high heat and add 6 patties. Cook for 8 minutes on each side or until brown, turning carefully. Remove and repeat with the remaining patties. Serve with the yoghurt, lettuce leaves and a squeeze of lime juice. **SERVES 4**

Sack of potatoes

Potatoes were the starch of the day when I was growing up. Pasta and rice barely got a look in; potatoes were definitely the people's favourite. Mum cooked potatoes for dinner every night of the week and it took me a while to come back to them when I started cooking for myself. The many beautiful and colourful varieties of the humble spud on the market today have won me over. And, while I'm not one to particularly bang the wooden spoon for organic food, you can make up your own mind: ah, yes, that's what a potato used to taste like.

WARM POTATO SALAD WITH SALMON AND CREME FRAICHE Just add smoked fish and creamy potato salad is transformed from a pleasing side-dish to a superstar. Use salmon or trout here, or my personal favourite: smoked mackerel.

1kg new potatoes
125ml buttermilk
3 tablespoons crème fraîche
1 tablespoon lemon juice
2 teaspoons Dijon mustard
3 tablespoons freshly
  snipped chives
3 tablespoons roughly chopped
  flat-leaf parsley
200g hot smoked salmon

Place the potatoes in a large saucepan of salted water and bring to the boil. Reduce heat and simmer gently for 15–20 minutes, or until tender. Drain well and set aside to cool.

To make the dressing, place the buttermilk, crème fraîche, lemon juice and mustard in a small bowl and whisk to combine. When the potatoes are cool enough to handle, cut each in half (or quarters if large) and place in a large bowl with the buttermilk dressing and season with sea salt. Toss to coat evenly then add the chives, parsley and smoked salmon. Toss once again very lightly and serve. **SERVES 4–6**

FONTINA TARTIFLETTE This is so Alpine I could almost break into a yodel. Tartiflette is often eaten by cross-country skiers who need plenty of carbs to keep up their strength. Does the school run count as strenuous exercise?

1.5kg waxy potatoes, peeled
15g unsalted butter
1 large onion, sliced
170g pancetta, diced
1 garlic clove, halved
250ml crème fraîche
500g ripe fontina cheese,
  rind on and thickly sliced
handful roughly chopped walnuts

Preheat the oven to 200°C/gas mark 6. Bring a large saucepan of water to the boil and cook the potatoes whole for 20–25 minutes, or until just tender. Drain and when cool enough to handle, cut into 1cm slices.

Meanwhile, melt the butter in a pan over medium heat and fry the onion for 5 minutes, or until soft. Transfer to a bowl. Add the pancetta to the pan and fry for 2–4 minutes, or until lightly golden. Remove with a slotted spoon and mix with the onion.

Rub a 25cm x 16cm ovenproof dish with the garlic. Lay half the potato slices in the base of the dish, season with freshly ground black pepper and a little sea salt (remembering the pancetta is salty), then scatter the onion mixture over the potato. Layer with the remaining potato and spread the crème fraîche over the top. Season well.

Evenly place the slices of fontina on top of the crème fraîche. Bake in the oven for 20–25 minutes, or until the top is lightly golden and the potato is cooked. Dress with chopped walnuts and serve immediately. **SERVES 4**

INDIAN SPICED POTATOES WITH FRIED EGG You know you're getting on when you just want an egg for dinner. Here's my attempt to step up that humble dish.

800g desiree potatoes,
   peeled and cut into 1cm dice
6 tablespoons sunflower oil
1 teaspoon black mustard seeds
2 garlic cloves, finely chopped
1 tablespoon finely chopped ginger
1 tablespoon medium-hot
   curry powder
½ teaspoon turmeric
25g unsalted butter
6 spring onions,
   trimmed and finely sliced
1 long green chilli, finely diced
   (deseeded, if liked)
½ teaspoon flaked sea salt
4 large eggs
small handful curry leaves

Bring a large saucepan of salted water to the boil over high heat. Add the potatoes, reduce to a simmer and cook for 13 minutes, or until just tender. Drain in a colander and leave to cool for a few minutes.

Place a non-stick frying pan over medium–high heat. Heat 2 tablespoons of the oil, sprinkle the mustard seeds into the pan and cook for a few seconds, or until just beginning to pop. Add the garlic, ginger, curry powder and turmeric and cook for 30 seconds, stirring constantly.

Drop the butter into the pan and as soon as it has melted, add another tablespoon of oil and the potatoes. Fry for 5 minutes, turning often. Scatter the spring onion, chilli and salt over the potatoes and toss together for a minute more. Season to taste and divide the potatoes among warmed plates.

In a clean large non-stick frying pan, add another tablespoon of oil and place over medium–high heat. Once hot, fry the eggs for 2–3 minutes until cooked. Meanwhile, fry the curry leaves in the remaining oil over medium–high heat for 2 minutes, until turning dark and glossy. Drain on kitchen paper.

Place the fried eggs on top of the potatoes and scatter with the curry leaves. **SERVES 4**

CHICKPEA, TOMATO AND SPINACH COTTAGE PIE Vegetarians often seem to miss out on the best comfort food, or just get handed a plate of chips and vegetables. If you've got a herbivore friend, serve this up and make their day.

2 tablespoons olive oil
1 red onion, halved and sliced
2 garlic cloves, crushed
1 red chilli, finely chopped
2 teaspoons ras el hanout
410g tin chopped tomatoes
400g tin chickpeas,
  drained and rinsed
250ml vegetable stock
1 tablespoon caster sugar
200g baby spinach leaves
1kg potatoes, peeled
  and cut into pieces
125g unsalted butter,
  roughly diced
1 tablespoon finely chopped
  coriander leaves
25g fresh breadcrumbs
15g freshly grated
  parmesan cheese

Preheat the oven to 200°C/gas mark 6. Heat the oil in a large frying pan over low heat and fry the onion for about 10 minutes, or until soft and beginning to caramelise. Add the garlic, chilli and ras el hanout and fry for 1 minute. Add the tomatoes, chickpeas, stock and sugar and season well with sea salt and freshly ground black pepper. Simmer for 15 minutes, or until the chickpeas are tender, stirring a few times to prevent the mixture sticking to the bottom of the pan. Add the spinach leaves to wilt. Spoon the mixture into four 10cm-diameter ovenproof dishes.

Meanwhile, bring a large saucepan of water to the boil. Add the potatoes and simmer for 20–30 minutes until they are tender. Drain and return to the heat for a few seconds to remove any excess water. Tip into a bowl, add the butter and mash until fluffy. Season to taste. Top each dish with the mashed potato.

Mix the coriander, breadcrumbs and parmesan in a small bowl and sprinkle over the top of each dish. Place on a large baking sheet and bake for 20 minutes, or until golden. Serve immediately. **SERVES 4**

POTATO, COURGETTE AND MOZZARELLA FRITTERS These fritters are so easy to make it's disgraceful. Serve them on their own with drinks, as a vegetable with grilled meats, or with a huge pile of bacon for a blow-out breakfast.

300g potatoes, coarsely grated
300g courgettes, coarsely grated
4 spring onions, chopped
125g grated mozzarella cheese
4 tablespoons roughly chopped
   flat-leaf parsley
2 eggs, lightly beaten
3 tablespoons plain flour
4 tablespoons light-flavoured oil
thick Greek yoghurt sprinkled
   with paprika
lemon wedges

Squeeze the grated potato and courgette to remove excess moisture. Place in a bowl with the spring onion, mozzarella, parsley and egg and stir lightly to combine. Stir in the flour and season with sea salt and freshly ground black pepper.

Heat the oil in a large non-stick frying pan over medium–high heat. Drop tablespoons of the mixture into the hot oil, flattening gently with the back of a spoon. Cook for 2 minutes on each side, or until golden brown. Drain on kitchen paper and serve with the yoghurt and lemon wedges. **MAKES 12**

BAKED JACKET POTATOES + KOHLRABI SLAW I never knew the charm of jacket potatoes before spending time in England. This makes a good Saturday lunch – best followed by an afternoon nap with the newspaper over your face.

4 large baking potatoes, scrubbed
1 tablespoon olive oil
unsalted butter
8–12 slices hand-carved ham

Preheat the oven to 180°C/gas mark 4. Rub the skins of the potatoes with the oil, place in a roasting tin and sprinkle with sea salt. Bake for 1¼ hours, or until the skins are blistered and the flesh is very soft and fluffy. Serve the potatoes with a knob of butter, the kohlrabi slaw and hand-carved ham. **SERVES 4**

KOHLRABI SLAW

3 medium kohlrabi, peeled,
   grated on a mandolin
   and squeezed to
   remove excess liquid
1 red onion, halved
   and thinly sliced
3 radishes, very finely
   sliced on a mandolin
4 tablespoons finely chopped
   flat-leaf parsley
3 tablespoons mayonnaise
2 tablespoons lemon juice
2 tablespoons baby capers

While the potatoes are baking, place the kohlrabi, onion and radish in a bowl and gently mix together. Add the parsley and season with sea salt and freshly ground black pepper. In a separate bowl, lightly whisk together the mayonnaise and lemon juice. Add the capers and season to taste.

Toss the dressing with the slaw and cover for 1 hour while the flavours develop and the vegetables soften.

Tin of beans

I'm a huge fan of fresh food, but there are a couple of tins I'd have to take with me to that desert island: tinned beans and tomatoes are the backbones of my kitchen. I was tickled pink when I read that Roman foot soldiers ate beans to keep them going as they conquered the world. What an advert for a humble foodstuff. If you want to soak dried beans overnight, please do. But I've got a short attention span and, by the time I've finished soaking and boiling, I've usually thought of something else I want to cook instead.

CROSTINI WITH WHITE BEANS + SALSA VERDE If having people over for dinner throws you into panic, try this easy dish for therapy. Serve with a light salad and white wine and you'll be laughing (but not hysterically, I hope).

1 loaf Italian bread, such
  as ciabatta, thinly sliced
2 tablespoons olive oil
2 garlic cloves, thinly sliced
finely grated zest 1 lemon
2 x 400g tins cannellini beans,
  drained and rinsed
80ml chicken or vegetable stock
extra-virgin olive oil, to drizzle
6–8 slices prosciutto
125g parmesan cheese,
  broken into chunks

Preheat the oven to 200°C/gas mark 6. Place the bread slices on two baking trays, drizzle with olive oil and season with sea salt and freshly ground black pepper. Bake for 10–12 minutes, until golden brown. Transfer to a serving platter and leave to cool.

For the white beans, put the 2 tablespoons olive oil, garlic and lemon zest in a saucepan and place over low heat. Cook for 2–3 minutes, until the garlic is softened but not coloured. Add the beans, stock, a pinch of salt and plenty of black pepper. Warm through for 3–4 minutes, tossing in the flavoured oil until hot. Remove from heat and lightly mash to roughly crush the beans (the bean mash will thicken as it cools). Tip into a serving bowl and leave to cool. Drizzle over extra-virgin olive oil and sprinkle generously with black pepper.

When ready to serve, place the bread, white beans, prosciutto, parmesan and salsa verde on a platter on the table for everyone to assemble their own crostini.
SERVES 4

SALSA VERDE

2 large handfuls flat-leaf parsley,
  finely shredded
small handful mint leaves,
  finely shredded
1 brown shallot, finely diced
90ml extra-virgin olive oil
60ml lemon juice
6 good-quality anchovy fillets
  in oil, finely chopped
2 tablespoons capers, rinsed,
  dried and chopped

Stir all the ingredients together in a bowl to combine and season with pepper only, to taste. The texture should be quite coarse. Transfer to a serving bowl.

SPICED CALAMARI AND CHICKPEAS This is a lovely salad on a summer evening.
I like to cook the calamari on the barbecue, but it's just as good done on the stove.

1kg calamari, cleaned, scored on
  the inside and cut into strips
4 tablespoons olive oil
1 teaspoon ras el hanout
2 tablespoons finely chopped
  preserved lemon
1 long green chilli, finely chopped
2 x 400g tins chickpeas,
  drained and rinsed
3 tablespoons roughly chopped
  coriander leaves
1 baby cos lettuce,
  leaves separated
1 lime, halved

Place the calamari, 2 tablespoons of the olive oil and
ras el hanout in a bowl and toss to combine. Preheat
a barbecue or chargrill pan on high heat. Cook the
calamari for 1–2 minutes each side, or until just
cooked. Don't overcook or it will be tough. Set aside.

In a saucepan over medium heat add the remaining
olive oil, preserved lemon and green chilli. Add the
chickpeas and warm through for 1–2 minutes, stirring.
Add the calamari and coriander and toss quickly.
Arrange the lettuce leaves on the serving plates,
and pile the calamari and chickpeas on top. Squeeze
over some lime juice and serve immediately. **SERVES 4**

WHITE BEAN SOUP This must be just about the quickest soup in the world. There
are almost no fresh ingredients to buy and it freezes well. What's not to love?

2 tablespoons olive oil
15g unsalted butter
2 medium onions, chopped
2 garlic cloves, finely chopped
½ teaspoon sea salt
1 rosemary sprig
4 x 400g tins cannellini beans,
  drained and rinsed
1 litre chicken stock
extra-virgin olive oil, to drizzle
handful rosemary leaves,
  roughly chopped

Heat the olive oil and butter in a large saucepan over
medium heat. When the butter has melted, add the
onion, garlic and salt. Cook for 8–10 minutes, stirring
occasionally, until the onion is soft and translucent.
Add the rosemary sprig, cannellini beans and chicken
stock. Bring to the boil then reduce the heat and
simmer for 10 minutes.

Remove the rosemary and purée the soup in a blender
or with a stick blender until smooth. Ladle into serving
bowls, drizzle with olive oil and dress with rosemary
leaves and freshly ground black pepper. **SERVES 4**

INDIVIDUAL BAKED BEANS WITH EGGS I've realised from my time spent in England that a humble tin of beans can elegantly cover all bases: breakfast, lunch and dinner. I've eaten this dish for all three (but not in the same day).

1 tablespoon olive oil
1 medium onion, finely chopped
100g pancetta, cubed
1 garlic clove, crushed
2 good-quality anchovies, chopped
1 teaspoon finely chopped
  thyme leaves
½ teaspoon dried oregano
1 teaspoon mild curry powder
400g tin chopped tomatoes
2 x 400g tins cannellini beans,
  drained and rinsed
4 eggs
handful flat-leaf parsley, torn

Preheat the oven to 190°C/gas mark 5. Heat the olive oil in a large frying pan over medium heat. Add the onion and fry, stirring occasionally, for 5 minutes, or until soft. Add the pancetta and garlic and fry until the pancetta is golden. Add the anchovies, thyme, oregano, curry powder and tomatoes. Cook until the sauce thickens, then add the cannellini beans and cook for a further 2–3 minutes, until the sauce coats the beans. Season to taste with sea salt and freshly ground black pepper.

Divide the beans into four 200ml ramekins. Carefully break a raw egg onto the piping hot mixture in each ramekin, cover with foil and place on a baking sheet. Bake for 15–20 minutes, or until the egg has just set. Dress with the parsley and a sprinkling of ground black pepper. Serve immediately. **SERVES 4**

CHICKPEA, BABY SPINACH AND PAN-FRIED PANEER SALAD Chickpeas and paneer cheese are an Indian duo usually cooked up together into a spicy vegetarian curry. Here's a summer salad for when you crave a hit of India without the curry.

1 bunch baby golden beetroot,
  stalks trimmed and scrubbed
400g tin chickpeas,
  drained and rinsed
3 garlic cloves, crushed
1 teaspoon cumin seeds
1 teaspoon dried chilli flakes
1 teaspoon paprika
3 tablespoons olive oil
300g paneer cheese,
  cut into chunks
100g baby spinach leaves
extra-virgin olive oil, to drizzle
1 lime
handful coriander sprigs

Preheat the oven to 180°C/gas mark 4. Place a saucepan of water over high heat and bring to the boil. Add the beetroot, reduce heat to a simmer and cook for 30 minutes, or until tender. Drain and when cool enough to handle, peel and cut in half.

Meanwhile, toss the chickpeas, garlic, cumin, chilli and paprika in 1 tablespoon of the olive oil and roast in the oven for 25–30 minutes, or until golden.

Place the remaining olive oil in a large non-stick frying pan and fry the paneer over medium heat until warmed through and browned on all sides. Arrange the spinach leaves, beetroot and cooked chickpeas on the serving plates. Drizzle each serving with olive oil and a squeeze of lime juice, season with sea salt and freshly ground black pepper and sprinkle with coriander leaves. Serve immediately. **SERVES 4**

MIXED BEAN CHILLI + CORN AND AVOCADO SALSA American friends in London served up bowls of chilli for Guy Fawkes Night – what a great idea! I love chilli, but my special favourites are those delicious extras: the salsas.

2 tablespoons olive oil
1 carrot, diced
1 medium onion, diced
2 celery sticks, diced
2 garlic cloves, chopped
1 tablespoon tomato purée
1–2 red chillies, finely chopped
1 teaspoon paprika
1 teaspoon ground cumin
½ teaspoon cayenne pepper
250ml vegetable stock
2 x 400g tins chopped tomatoes
1 tablespoon caster sugar
2 x 400g tins mixed beans,
  rinsed and drained
soured cream sprinkled
  with paprika
1 ripe avocado, halved
grated cheese
crispy tortillas

Place the olive oil in an ovenproof casserole dish over low heat and cook the carrot, onion and celery for 10 minutes, until starting to soften. Add the garlic, tomato purée, chilli, spices and stock and cook for 1 minute more. Add the tomatoes, sugar and beans, then cover and simmer for 30 minutes. Remove the lid and cook for a further 15 minutes.

Serve the beans with separate bowls of the corn and avocado salsa, soured cream, avocado, grated cheese and crispy tortillas so everyone can make their own tortillas. **SERVES 4**

CORN AND AVOCADO SALSA

2 fresh corn cobs
3 brown shallots, finely sliced
1 large avocado, roughly diced
1 teaspoon sesame oil
2 tablespoons lime juice
2 teaspoons sambal oelek
1 teaspoon caster sugar

Cut the kernels off the cobs and blanch in a saucepan of boiling water for 1 minute, until bright yellow and cooked. Refresh under cold water and drain well. Place in a large bowl with the shallot and avocado.

Combine the sesame oil, lime juice, sambal oelek and sugar in a small bowl and stir until the sugar has dissolved. Gently toss through the salad and season with sea salt and freshly ground black pepper.

BAKED AUBERGINE, CHICKPEAS AND GREEN CHILLI Pomegranate seeds always take me back to the magical fruit of *Grimm's Fairy Tales*. This is a fantastic vegetarian main course. Rev up the protein by sprinkling with feta when serving.

3 aubergines, cut lengthways
　　into 1cm-thick slices
4 tablespoons olive oil
1 medium onion, finely chopped
3 garlic cloves, crushed
1 tablespoon grated ginger
1 green chilli, finely diced
2 teaspoons paprika
1 teaspoon ground cumin
400g tin chopped tomatoes
400g tin chickpeas,
　　rinsed and drained
2 tablespoons pomegranate
　　molasses (or 1 tablespoon
　　light brown sugar mixed with
　　1 tablespoon lemon juice)
1 tablespoon chopped
　　flat-leaf parsley
1 tablespoon chopped mint leaves
2 tablespoons pomegranate seeds

Preheat the oven to 180°C/gas mark 4. Sprinkle the aubergine slices with salt, place in a colander and leave for 20 minutes. Rinse well and pat dry with kitchen paper.

Place two large frying pans over medium–high heat. Lightly brush both sides of the aubergine slices with olive oil. Add a single layer in each pan and fry for 4–6 minutes on both sides, until well browned. Set aside and repeat with the remaining aubergine. Place half the aubergine slices in a medium casserole dish.

Return a frying pan to the heat with 1 tablespoon olive oil. Add the onion, garlic, ginger, chilli, paprika and cumin, and cook, stirring occasionally, until the onion is translucent. Add the tomatoes, chickpeas and pomegranate molasses. Mix together and season well with sea salt and freshly ground black pepper.

Pour half the tomato mixture over the aubergine slices in the casserole dish, cover with the remaining aubergine and then pour over the remaining tomato. Transfer to the oven and bake for 15 minutes.

Serve in the dish or allow to rest and serve warm or at room temperature dressed with parsley and mint, pomegranate seeds and sea salt. **SERVES 4-6**

Slice of cheese

Given the choice between cheese and dessert, I'll always pick the cheese. I like it even better as I age – in the same way as a good stilton, I like to think. Hot, bubbling molten cheese is my comfort food, whether grilled on bread, baked into flaky pastry or melted over pasta. Incidentally, I'd like you to know that chefs have no more luck than anyone else in persuading their kids to eat something they don't want to. My daughter Inès hates cheese with a passion. A fondue night while on an idyllic holiday in Switzerland is now entrenched in this family's folklore as our horror evening of all time.

ANTIPASTO PLATE WITH FRIED BOCCONCINI BALLS Invite friends for drinks and make your bocconcini the centrepiece of a big antipasto platter. Just don't tell anyone you're serving fried balls of cheese – it can be our secret.

16 bocconcini
200g breadcrumbs
3 medium eggs, beaten
50g plain flour
light-flavoured oil, for deep-frying
300g saucisson (or other cured salami), cut into chunks
200g marinated artichoke hearts, roughly chopped
3 medium tomatoes, chopped

Place the bocconcini on kitchen paper and pat dry. Spread the breadcrumbs on a large plate and have the eggs ready in a separate bowl. Place the flour in a bowl and season well with sea salt and freshly ground black pepper. Dip a bocconcini into the flour and shake off any excess, then coat in egg and roll in the breadcrumbs. Repeat this once more, so the bocconcini is evenly coated. Place on a plate and keep chilled. Repeat with the remaining bocconcini.

Heat the oil in a deep-fryer or a high-sided pan to 190°C or until a cube of bread dropped into the oil browns within 30 seconds. Deep-fry the bocconcini balls, a few at a time, for 1–2 minutes or until golden and crisp. Remove and drain on kitchen paper. Once all the balls are cooked, season well and serve immediately on an antipasto plate with the saucisson, artichoke hearts and tomatoes. **SERVES 4**

RICOTTA AND SPINACH GNUDI WITH SAGE BUTTER While gnocchi means 'dumplings' in Italian, gnudi means, well, 'nude'. These ricotta and spinach balls are ravioli filling without the pasta wrappers. Buy best-quality ricotta in the wheel.

400g baby spinach leaves
350g ricotta cheese
50g finely grated parmesan cheese
1 egg, plus 2 egg yolks, lightly beaten
1 tablespoon plain flour, plus extra for dusting
100g unsalted butter, chopped
20 small sage leaves

Place the spinach in a large frying pan with a splash of water and cook over medium heat until wilted. Drain and squeeze out as much water as possible. Roughly chop the spinach, transfer to a large bowl and combine with the cheeses, egg, flour, sea salt and freshly ground black pepper. Flour your hands to shape the mixture into 4cm-diameter balls (about 1 tablespoon of mixture each).

Bring a large saucepan of salted water to the boil and cook 8 or so gnudi at a time. When they rise to the surface after a minute or so, cook for an extra minute then remove with a slotted spoon to a warm bowl.

Melt the butter in a small frying pan over medium heat. Add the sage leaves and cook, swirling the pan often, for 4–5 minutes, until the sage is crisp and the butter has turned a deep nut-brown. Season well.

Divide the gnudi into the serving bowls and spoon over the sage butter. **SERVES 4 (MAKES 32)**

SHORTCRUST CHEESE TART Enjoy this tart at room temperature with tomatoes as a summer lunch, or hot from the oven with bitter greens in winter. This is an easy shortcrust pastry, but if you're rushed off your feet use shop-bought.

1 quantity shortcrust pastry
100g feta cheese, crumbled
250g ricotta cheese
200g mature cheddar, grated
2 eggs, lightly beaten
3 tablespoons double cream
pinch freshly ground nutmeg
1 tablespoon coarsely chopped
   rosemary leaves
1 egg yolk, lightly beaten

Preheat the oven to 180°C/gas mark 4. Place the pastry dough on a lightly floured surface and roll out to a circle about 35cm in diameter. Transfer to a lightly floured baking tray.

Place the cheeses, beaten egg, cream, nutmeg and a pinch of freshly ground black pepper in a bowl and mix well. Spoon onto the centre of the dough and spread evenly, leaving a 5cm border around the edge. Use your hands to lift and fold the pastry border over the filling. Sprinkle the rosemary over the top of the tart, brush the pastry with the egg yolk and chill for 15–20 minutes. Bake for 45–50 minutes until the filling is set and the pastry is golden (cover loosely with foil if the tart is browning too quickly).

SERVES 4–6

SHORTCRUST PASTRY

385g plain flour
½ teaspoon salt
170g chilled unsalted butter,
   cut into small pieces
4 tablespoons chilled water

Place the flour, salt and butter in a food processor and blend to a fine breadcrumb consistency. Add the chilled water and pulse until only just starting to come together. Turn out, press the mixture together, wrap in cling film and refrigerate for 30 minutes.

BLUE CHEESE AND PANCETTA TRAY LOAF I always think that if you're going to bother making your own bread, you don't want to do much else, so make it a meal in itself. If you can't help over-achieving, serve with the white bean soup, page 173.

600g strong white flour
1 teaspoon sea salt
1 tablespoon caster sugar
1 tablespoon dried instant yeast
100ml olive oil, plus extra
    2 tablespoons for frying
3 large onions, sliced
1 tablespoon thyme leaves
1 teaspoon caster sugar
1 tablespoon balsamic vinegar
50g pancetta, sliced
2–3 tablespoons rosemary leaves,
    plus extra to serve
extra-virgin olive oil, to drizzle
125g blue cheese, crumbled

Place the flour, salt, 1 tablespoon caster sugar and yeast in a bowl and mix. Create a well in the middle and add 300ml warm water and 100ml olive oil. Bring the mixture together to a soft dough and turn out onto a lightly floured surface. Knead for 10 minutes until smooth and elastic. Place in a lightly oiled bowl, cover with a tea towel and leave to rise in a warm place for 1 hour.

Heat the 2 tablespoons olive oil in a frying pan over medium heat and cook the onion and thyme for 25 minutes until soft and golden. Add 1 teaspoon caster sugar and the vinegar and cook for a further 3 minutes. Season with salt and freshly ground black pepper and set aside. Wipe out the pan and return to the heat. Add the pancetta and rosemary and cook until crisp. Remove and set aside in a separate bowl.

Knock back the dough to its original size by punching with your fist then stretch out into a long oval shape. Place on a lightly oiled baking tray, cover with a damp tea towel and leave to rise for 30 minutes.

Preheat the oven to 220°C/gas mark 7. Make random dimples in the surface of the dough with your fingertips. Top with the caramelised onion, a good drizzle of extra-virgin olive oil and salt. Bake for 20 minutes, or until golden brown.

Remove the tray loaf and sprinkle with blue cheese, pancetta and rosemary. Bake for an extra 2 minutes until the cheese just begins to melt. Dress with extra rosemary leaves and serve immediately. **SERVES 4–6**

FETA AND GRUYERE PASTRIES + SPICY TOMATO RELISH These pastries are my daughter Bunny's absolute favourite food. We first had them in Greece, but I've added a hint of cultural cross-pollination with this spicy Indian-style relish.

2 large eggs, lightly beaten
100g gruyère cheese, grated
100g feta cheese, crumbled
4 sheets filo pastry from
  250g packet, thawed
80g unsalted butter, melted
paprika, to dust

Preheat the oven to 180°C/gas mark 4. Grease a baking tray with a little melted butter.

To make the filling, combine the beaten egg, cheeses and freshly ground black pepper in a bowl. Set aside.

Cut the pastry sheets lengthways into 10cm-wide strips. Brush with melted butter, fold over lengthways and butter again, and place a tablespoon of filling on the end. Fold one corner right to left to create a triangle, and then left to right to reinforce the triangle, and repeat until you have a filled triangle. Butter the outside of the pastry, sprinkle with paprika and bake for 20 minutes, or until golden.

You can freeze the pastries if you would like to prepare ahead. Defrost for 2 hours before baking.
MAKES 12

SPICY TOMATO RELISH

400g tin chopped tomatoes
1 teaspoon turmeric
1 tablespoon finely grated ginger
2 garlic cloves, crushed
2 tablespoons soft brown sugar
2 tablespoons red wine vinegar
2 green chillies, finely diced
3 tablespoons olive oil

Place all the ingredients in a small saucepan over medium–high heat. Season with sea salt and freshly ground black pepper, bring to the boil, then drop to a gentle simmer and cook for 30 minutes. Transfer to a bowl and allow to cool before serving.

RICOTTA AND PARMESAN LASAGNA This is simple cheese and pasta – a sort of 'naked' lasagna. Serve it with a nutty side salad to guarantee plenty of crunch.

80g unsalted butter
1 brown shallot, finely chopped
75g plain flour
1 litre skimmed milk
3 large bay leaves
500g ricotta cheese
12–15 fresh or precooked
    dried lasagna sheets
50g finely grated
    parmesan cheese

Preheat the oven to 200°C/gas mark 6. Lightly grease a large ovenproof dish or roasting tin.

To make the cheese sauce, melt the butter in a large saucepan over medium heat. Cook the shallot for 1–2 minutes, stirring, until softened. Sprinkle the flour into the pan and cook for 30 seconds, stirring.

Gradually stir in the milk, then add 1 bay leaf and bring to a gentle simmer. Cook for 5 minutes, stirring constantly, until the sauce is thickened and smooth. If the sauce starts to get lumpy, swap your spoon for a balloon whisk. Remove from the heat, discard the bay leaf and stir in the ricotta. Season with plenty of sea salt and freshly ground black pepper.

Spoon a quarter of the sauce into the base of the buttered dish or tin and top with a layer of lasagna sheets. Repeat the layers twice more, finishing with a layer of cheese sauce. Sprinkle with the parmesan. Bake for 35–40 minutes, until golden and bubbling. Place the remaining bay leaves on top of the lasagna 5 minutes before the end of cooking. **SERVES 4–6**

Carton of eggs

Like the rest of the world, it seems, Natalie has decided we need to get a chicken coop and chickens to live in it. In the seventies, gardens had Astroturf; in the eighties, it was the Tuscan-tiled pergola; in the nineties, the water feature was king; and now, in the 21st century, there are chickens clucking in gardens from Bondi to Islington. A good egg with a golden yolk – especially one freshly laid in your own back yard – is a beautiful thing, and something I find more appealing as I get older. I never thought I'd write another recipe for scrambled eggs, but there's one here: most likely not the one you're expecting, though.

NORTHERN CHINESE SCRAMBLED EGGS I honestly thought I'd covered all bases with scrambled eggs, until I wandered into my first northern Chinese restaurant. This is such a crazy-delicious flavour combination.

6 large eggs
1 teaspoon Szechuan pepper
1 teaspoon sea salt,
  plus extra pinch
2 tablespoons light-flavoured oil
6 spring onions, finely chopped
1 small garlic clove, crushed
3 medium tomatoes,
  cut into chunks
1 teaspoon sugar
small handful watercress
steamed rice (see page 35)

Whisk the eggs with a pinch of sea salt and freshly ground black pepper until smooth. To make Szechuan salt, roughly crush the Szechuan pepper with a mortar and pestle, add the salt and crush together.

Heat 1 tablespoon of the oil in a non-stick wok over medium–high heat. Add the egg mixture and swirl the pan on the heat for 30 seconds, or until lightly browned around the outer edge but still liquid in the centre. Transfer to a large bowl.

Heat the remaining oil in the wok. Add the spring onion and garlic and stir-fry for 30 seconds, or until just softened. Add the tomatoes and sugar and cook, stirring occasionally, until just softened but still whole. Return the eggs to the wok and fold gently until just set. Remove from the heat and leave for a few seconds. Sprinkle with the Szechuan salt and serve with the watercess and steamed rice. **SERVES 2**

EGGS WITH ARTICHOKES AND TOMATOES This is my version of the Italian classic 'eggs in purgatory'. (Surely only someone harbouring a great deal of Catholic guilt could refer to an innocent eggy supper as 'in purgatory'?)

2 tablespoons olive oil
100g pancetta, chopped
1 red onion, sliced
2 x 400g tins chopped tomatoes
280g jar artichoke hearts,
  quartered
8 eggs
½ teaspoon dried chilli flakes
handful flat-leaf parsley, chopped

Place a large frying pan over medium–high heat. Add the oil and pancetta and cook for 4–5 minutes, until lightly browned. Add the onion and cook for a further 4–5 minutes, or until softened. Add the tomatoes, season with sea salt and freshly ground black pepper and cook for 10–12 minutes, until slightly reduced. Add the artichoke hearts, mix to combine, and reduce heat to medium–low.

Make 8 divots in the tomato mixture with the back of a spoon and break an egg into each one. Cook for 4–5 minutes, or until the whites are opaque and the yolks are still soft. Sprinkle with a little dried chilli and parsley and season to taste. **SERVES 4**

LEEK AND SPINACH CAKE This is a delicious green savoury cake, packed full of spinach and eggs – very healthy and very clean. Of course, if you want, you could ruin all that by serving it with a pile of crispy bacon.

1 tablespoon olive oil
15g unsalted butter
2 leeks, chopped
200g baby spinach leaves or
　watercress, stems removed
pinch grated nutmeg
125ml milk
6 large eggs, lightly beaten
25g freshly grated
　parmesan cheese
handful watercress, to serve

Preheat the oven to 180°C/gas mark 4 and grease a medium (about 800ml) round ovenproof dish.

Heat the oil and butter in a saucepan over medium heat. Add the leek and cook gently for about 10 minutes, until soft. Add the spinach and the nutmeg and season with sea salt and freshly ground black pepper. Cover and leave to wilt for 5 minutes. Remove the spinach, increase the heat and reduce the liquid in the pan to about 1 tablespoon.

Transfer the spinach and liquid to a food processor. Add the milk and beaten egg and blend until smooth but still slightly textured. Pour into the prepared ovenproof dish and scatter with the parmesan. Bake for 25–30 minutes, until golden brown. Serve topped with watercress. **SERVES 4**

POACHED EGGS WITH LENTIL, BACON AND ROCKET SALAD The trick here is to cook your egg to exactly the right degree: a firm white and free-flowing golden yolk that runs over the lentils, bacon and rocket, coating everything in its path.

150g dried Puy lentils
4 slices middle bacon,
  rind removed and chopped
2 tablespoons red wine vinegar
1 garlic clove, crushed
4 very fresh free-range eggs
1 bunch chives, finely chopped
extra-virgin olive oil, to drizzle
60g wild rocket
2 tablespoons chervil leaves

Place the lentils in a saucepan with 500ml water and bring to the boil over high heat. Reduce heat to medium and simmer for 20–25 minutes, until the lentils are tender. Strain and set aside.

Place a large frying pan over medium–high heat and cook the bacon, stirring, until well browned. Add the cooked lentils, red wine vinegar and garlic and cook for 2 minutes. Set aside.

In a shallow frying pan, bring 5cm of water to the boil. Turn off the heat and add the eggs at once. To minimise the spreading of the whites, break the eggs directly into the water, carefully opening the two halves of the shells at the water surface so they slide into the water. Cover the pan with a tight-fitting lid and leave them to cook undisturbed for about 3 minutes. The eggs are cooked when the whites are opaque. Remove them from the pan with a slotted spoon and drain on a clean tea towel. Using a small knife, gently trim away the thin outer layer of egg white around the edge.

Toss the lentils with the chives and arrange on the serving plates. Top each with a poached egg, drizzle with olive oil and add rocket, chervil and ground black pepper. **SERVES 4**

BAKED EGGS WITH THREE CHEESES What could be more comforting on a cold winter evening than your own little pot of molten cheese covered by a golden crust of creamy egg? Served with toast soldiers for dunking would be even better.

15g unsalted butter
1 leek, halved lengthways
  and cut into 1cm slices
125g buffalo mozzarella, diced
125g goat's cheese, crumbled
80g coarsely grated
  parmesan cheese
6 large eggs, lightly beaten
125ml double cream

Preheat the oven to 200°C/gas mark 6. Melt the butter in a pan and gently sauté the leek for about 5 minutes, until soft. Divide the leek into 4 shallow 250ml ovenproof dishes and sprinkle with the three cheeses. Whisk together the eggs and cream, season with sea salt and freshly ground black pepper and pour over the top.

Bake for 15–20 minutes, until puffed and dark golden. Serve immediately. **SERVES 4**

SPANISH TORTILLA Don't get your tortillas muddled: there's the Mexican bread-like tortilla and the Spanish omelette – the tortilla *de patatas*. Potatoes, peppers, onions and chorizo are the traditional fillings of the Spanish tortilla.

100ml olive oil, plus extra to brush
700g potatoes (such as desiree),
  peeled, thinly sliced, patted dry
2 white onions, thinly sliced
1 red pepper, deseeded
  and thinly sliced
175g chorizo, diced
9 large eggs
2 tablespoons chopped
  flat-leaf parsley
tomato relish (shop bought)
large handful rocket leaves

Heat half the olive oil in a medium (about 26cm) non-stick frying pan. Lay the potato slices in the pan and cook, turning occasionally, for 10 minutes, until golden and almost tender. Remove from the pan and place in a large bowl. Return the pan to the heat and add the remaining oil, onions, pepper and chorizo. Cook, stirring occasionally, for 6–7 minutes, until the onions and chorizo are light golden. Remove and add to the potato mixture.

Whisk the eggs together, add the parsley and season with sea salt and freshly ground black pepper. Pour over the potato mixture.

Wipe out the frying pan with kitchen paper, brush with olive oil and place over medium heat. Carefully pour the combined mixture into the pan, evenly distributing the potato, onion, pepper and chorizo. Reduce the heat to very low, cover with foil and cook for 20 minutes, or until almost set.

Preheat the grill to high. Place the pan under the grill and cook for 4–8 minutes, until set and golden. Remove and allow to cool for 5 minutes before turning out onto a clean chopping board. Cut into wedges and serve with tomato relish and rocket leaves. The tortilla can also be served cold. **SERVES 6**

Apples + pears

I've always loved a cold, juicy apple straight from the fridge on a hot day in Sydney. And a perfectly ripe pear, thinly sliced and eaten with cheese and honey, is of those little pleasures that can brighten a grim Monday. Since spending more time in England, I've come to appreciate apples and pears as cold-climate autumn fruit with their own place in the season of the fruit bowl. When that season's over, don't risk a moment of disappointment biting into a floury apple. Apples caramelised in pastry and ripe pears poached in wine – so easily done, it's ridiculous.

QUICK BIRCHER MUESLI + SPICED CRANBERRIES When I first made this I would soak the apples overnight, but finely slicing them works just as well and is super quick. My daughters love this, which is great because I know how healthy it is.

150g quick-cook rolled oats
250ml milk
250g Greek yoghurt
1 teaspoon vanilla extract
1 tablespoon honey
3 apples, finely sliced
   into matchsticks
   (easy with a mandolin)
50g whole almonds, lightly
   toasted and roughly chopped

Mix together the oats, milk, yoghurt, vanilla extract and honey and leave to sit for 10 minutes or longer to soften. Divide into serving bowls and top with the apple. Add more milk if a thinner consistency is preferred. Sprinkle with the almonds and serve with the spiced cranberries. **SERVES 4–6**

SPICED CRANBERRIES

110g caster sugar
100ml freshly squeezed
   orange juice
1 cinnamon stick
300g cranberries, fresh or frozen

Place the sugar and orange juice in a non-reactive saucepan over low heat and slowly dissolve the sugar. Add the cinnamon stick and bring the syrup up to the boil. Add the cranberries and cook for 1–2 minutes, until they soften but still hold their shape. Remove with a slotted spoon and place in a serving bowl.

Return the syrup to the heat, bring to the boil and cook until reduced by half. Discard the cinnamon stick and pour the hot syrup over the cranberries. Set aside until needed.

MALVA PUDDING + BUTTERED PEARS I recently worked in South Africa with chef Justin Boncllo. This is his recipe, and it will forever remind me of giraffes and zebra cantering elegantly across the safari parks.

95g unsalted butter
1 tablespoon apricot jam
250ml milk
150g plain flour
1 teaspoon baking powder
220g caster sugar
1 egg
1 teaspoon white wine vinegar
2 teaspoons vanilla extract
180ml double cream
110g soft brown sugar

Preheat the oven to 180°C/gas mark 4 and grease four 250ml ramekins or ovenproof cups.

Place 15g of the butter in a small saucepan with the jam and milk and heat gently until the butter melts. Cool slightly.

Sieve the flour and baking powder into a large bowl and set aside. In another bowl whisk together the sugar and egg until light and fluffy. Continue whisking while adding the vinegar and 1 teaspoon vanilla extract, then the milk mixture. Fold in the flour until well combined. Pour into the greased ramekins and bake for 25–30 minutes, until cooked and golden.

Meanwhile, prepare the sauce. Place the remaining butter and vanilla extract with the cream and sugar in a medium saucepan and heat gently until the sugar has dissolved, taking care not to let boil or the sauce will split. Set aside.

Remove the puddings from the oven. Use a teaspoon to make a hole in the centre of each one and wiggle the spoon from side to side to create a well. Pour 1–2 tablespoons of the sauce into each pudding. Return the puddings to the oven for a further 10–15 minutes. Serve with the buttered pears and extra sauce on the side. **SERVES 6**

BUTTERED PEARS

30g unsalted butter
1 tablespoon caster sugar
3 firm ripe pears,
  cored and quartered
2 tablespoons honey
1 vanilla pod, split and
  seeds scraped out

Place the butter and sugar in a frying pan and melt over medium heat. Add the pears, honey, vanilla pod and seeds. Cover and cook gently for about 20 minutes, until the undersides of the pears are pale golden. Turn the pears over very gently to avoid breaking them, and cook until golden. Serve warm.

FREE-FORM APPLE TART This is my favourite sort of dish: it looks spectacular but is dead easy. The tart case can be as messy as you like and you still can't go wrong — any combination of pastry, sugar and apples is destined to taste great.

225g plain flour
150g unsalted butter, cubed
1 egg yolk
2 tablespoons iced water
5 medium apples (cox or
   granny smith), halved,
   cored and thinly sliced
55g demerara sugar
½ teaspoon ground cinnamon
icing sugar, to dust

To make the pastry, process the flour, butter cubes and a pinch of sea salt together in a food processor until the mixture resembles coarse breadcrumbs. Add the egg yolk and iced water and pulse until the dough forms a ball. Wrap in cling film and chill in the fridge for a minimum 30 minutes.

Preheat the oven to 180°C/gas mark 4. Lightly dust a work surface with flour. Roll the pastry out into a 30cm x 20cm rectangle and place on a baking tray. Arrange the apple slices in rows on top, sprinkle with the sugar and cinnamon and bake for 40–45 minutes, until the apples are golden (cover loosely with foil if they are browning too quickly). Serve dusted with icing sugar. **SERVES 4**

GINGER PEAR UPSIDE-DOWN PUDDING The upside-down pudding has to be one of the greatest cooking inventions. However uneven your chopping, it's all hidden away in the bottom of a dish with a beautiful golden sponge puffed up on top.

5 ripe pears,
   cored and quartered
3 tablespoons orange juice
50g demerara sugar
2 large eggs
220g caster sugar
150g plain flour
1 teaspoon ground ginger,
   plus extra to dust
2 teaspoons baking powder
4 tablespoons soured cream
125g unsalted butter, melted
1 teaspoon vanilla extract
icing sugar, to dust
single cream, to serve

Preheat the oven to 180°C/gas mark 4. Grease an 18cm ovenproof deep-sided ceramic dish or frying pan. Place the pears, orange juice and demerara sugar in the pan and gently toss together.

In a large bowl, beat together the eggs and caster sugar with electric beaters until pale and creamy. Sift the flour, ginger and baking powder over the mixture and lightly beat until smooth. Fold in the soured cream, butter and vanilla. Spoon over the pears in the pan, smoothing the surface with a spatula.

Bake for 45–50 minutes, or until a skewer inserted into the centre comes out clean. Leave to cool for 5 minutes. Dust with icing sugar and the extra ground ginger and serve warm with cream. **SERVES 4–6**

APPLE AND VANILLA TURNOVERS The apple turnover was a traditional autumn pudding in England – all those apples in careful layers, stocked in the outhouse to 'see you through the winter'. Now you can make them all year round. Try adding a handful of summer berries to the filling when the sun is shining.

25g unsalted butter
1kg granny smith apples, peeled,
  cored and cut into chunks
3 tablespoons caster sugar
1 teaspoon vanilla extract
2 x 375g ready-rolled puff
  pastry sheets
3 tablespoons demerara sugar
1 egg, beaten
vanilla ice-cream, to serve

Preheat the oven to 200°C/gas mark 6. Melt the butter in a frying pan over medium–high heat. Add the apple and cook for 10 minutes, stirring regularly. Sprinkle over the caster sugar and vanilla extract. Cook for 15 minutes, stirring frequently, until the apple has taken on a nice golden colour. Remove from the heat and leave to cool completely.

Line 2 baking sheets with baking paper and sprinkle with half the demerara sugar. If necessary, roll out each pastry sheet until roughly 25cm x 35cm. Cut six 11cm rounds from each pastry sheet. If the pastry softens so that it becomes unmanageable, just place it in the fridge until it firms. Lightly brush the edge of each round with the beaten egg, place a spoonful of apple near the centre and then fold one side of the pastry over to make a half-circle shape. Press around the edge with a fork to seal each turnover.

Make 3 slashes on the top of each turnover, place on the baking sheets and brush with the beaten egg. Sprinkle with the remaining sugar and place in the fridge for 20 minutes for the pastry to firm up.

Bake in the hot oven for 10 minutes, then reduce heat to 180°C/gas mark 4 and bake for a further 10–15 minutes, until the pastry is golden and cooked through. Serve with vanilla ice-cream. **MAKES 12**

Punnet of berries

My new weekend hobby is blackberrying. In Australia, poking around in bushes in the countryside can be fraught with anxiety over what poisonous creature might lunge out to take a bite, so we wear gumboots and stamp our feet in constant warning. In England, we need only worry about speeding locals, who force us to hurl ourselves into ditches to avoid the wheels of their Range Rovers. As I've said so often (do I protest too much?), I don't have a sweet tooth, but I love berry desserts. I can use chocolate, sugar and cream and know that the quick-tempered tartness of the berries will cut through any cloying sweetness.

BLACKBERRY JELLY + VANILLA ICE-CREAM Here's an amazing fact a lot of people (especially small children) don't believe. You can make your own jelly from fresh fruit rather than a packet. And it tastes like fruit. Really.

150g blackberries
150g caster sugar
2 teaspoons gelatine powder

Place the blackberries, sugar and 200ml water in a small saucepan and heat gently over low–medium heat until the sugar is dissolved and the blackberries are soft. Mash the blackberries with the back of a wooden spoon then push the mixture through a fine sieve into a measuring jug. Add more hot water to the jug so that the total liquid quantity is 500ml.

Return the liquid to a clean saucepan and sprinkle over the gelatine. Place over low heat and stir until the gelatine has dissolved. Remove from heat and allow to cool for a few minutes, then pour into four 125ml glasses or bowls and chill for 4 hours or until set. Serve with the vanilla ice-cream. **SERVES 4**

VANILLA ICE-CREAM

220g caster sugar
600ml double cream
2 teaspoons vanilla extract
1 tablespoon lemon juice
480g soured cream

In a large bowl whisk together the sugar, cream, vanilla extract and lemon juice with electric beaters until soft peaks form and the mixture is still pourable (do not reach stiff peaks as the resulting ice-cream will have ice crystals).

Gently fold through the soured cream until well combined. Transfer to a shallow tub and freeze for a minimum 4 hours, or until the ice-cream is solid. Remove from the freezer about 15 minutes before serving to allow to soften.

STRAWBERRY PANNACOTTA Look at these beautiful little pale pink puddings on the plate. Sometimes I think it shows in my cooking that I live with four girls.

400g strawberries, plus extra
    200g strawberries freshly
    hulled, diced and tossed
    in icing sugar, to serve
250g plain yoghurt
185ml double cream
55g caster sugar
4 leaves gelatine

Blend the 400g strawberries and yoghurt in a food processor until smooth. Strain the mixture through a sieve to remove the seeds.

Place the cream and sugar in a pan and bring to a simmer over low heat, stirring to dissolve the sugar. Soak the gelatine in cold water until soft. Squeeze out the excess water, drop the leaves into the hot cream and stir until completely dissolved. Remove from heat and quickly stir in the strawberry mixture. Divide among six 125ml plastic dariole moulds, cover with cling film and chill for 8 hours or overnight.

To remove from the moulds, dip them into hot water for a couple of seconds and then invert onto a plate. Top each pannacotta with the additional diced strawberries and serve immediately. **SERVES 4**

BLACKBERRY AND PLUM STREUSEL CAKE In America they call this a coffee cake and serve it for breakfast. I can't begin to imagine how much I'd weigh if I did that.

300g plain flour
30g unsalted butter, chilled
    and cut into small cubes
1½ tablespoons soft brown sugar
2 teaspoons baking powder
125g unsalted butter, softened
220g caster sugar
3 eggs
235g soured cream
350g plums, halved and stoned
250g blackberries
single cream, to serve

Preheat the oven to 170°C/gas mark 3. Lightly grease a 22cm-square cake tin and line with baking paper, letting the paper overhang slightly around the rim to assist with removing the streusel once cooked.

To make the topping, place 50g of the flour in a bowl, add the cold cubed butter and rub in until the mixture resembles coarse breadcrumbs. Mix in the brown sugar and set aside.

To make the cake, sift the remaining flour, the baking powder and a pinch of sea salt into a bowl. In a large bowl, cream the softened butter and caster sugar with electric beaters. Add the eggs, one at a time, beating well after each addition. Add the dry ingredients, alternating with the soured cream, while being careful not to over-mix (some small lumps of flour are OK). Pour the batter into the lined cake tin and sprinkle with the plums, 150g of the blackberries and the topping. Bake for 55–60 minutes, or until a skewer inserted into the centre comes out clean.

Allow to cool a little before lifting out of the tin. Serve warm or at room temperature with the remaining blackberries and cream. **SERVES 8**

WHITE CHOCOLATE AND BLUEBERRY CHEESECAKE | first made a chocolate cheesecake many years ago for *bills food* and over time the recipe has evolved. I've left out the sugar in the filling here: the white chocolate is sweet enough and this way you can enjoy the sourness of the cheese.

200g plain sweet biscuits
100g unsalted butter, melted
250g cream cheese, softened
500g mascarpone cheese
500g white chocolate, melted
3 x 125g punnets blueberries,
   plus extra blueberries, to serve
60ml orange juice
2 tablespoons caster sugar
½ teaspoon vanilla paste

Lightly grease and line a 20cm-round spring form tin with baking paper. Process the biscuits in a food processor until they resemble breadcrumbs. Add the melted butter, process to combine then transfer to the prepared tin. Press the mixture firmly into the base of the tin, then chill in the fridge until needed.

Use electric beaters to beat the cream cheese, mascarpone and chocolate together until smooth. Pour over the prepared base and smooth the surface. Cover the tin with cling film and chill overnight to set.

Place 2 punnets of the blueberries in a small frying pan over low–meduim heat. Add the orange juice, sugar and vanilla paste and simmer until the berries are starting to break down. Remove from heat, add the remaining punnet of blueberries and stir gently.

To serve, carefully remove the collar of the tin (you may need to run a small sharp knife around the edge to loosen), and remove the base. Place the cheesecake on a serving plate and spoon over the berry sauce. Top with extra blueberries. **SERVES 8**

LEMON PUDDING CAKE WITH BERRIES I once heard this described as a 'late summer cake' — that's somewhere between a sponge cake and a winter pudding.

2 x 125g punnets raspberries
75g plain flour
2 teaspoons baking powder
pinch sea salt
300ml buttermilk
125g unsalted butter, melted and
 cooled, plus extra for greasing
3 eggs, separated
150g caster sugar
2 teaspoons finely grated
 lemon zest
icing sugar, to dust

Preheat the oven to 180°C/gas mark 4. Grease a 750ml–1 litre shallow baking dish, ensuring you have a larger baking dish this dish can fit into. Scatter the raspberries over the base of the greased dish.

Combine the flour, baking powder and salt in a large bowl. Lightly whisk together the buttermilk, butter, egg yolks, sugar and lemon zest in a separate bowl, then stir into the flour mixture.

Beat the egg whites with electric beaters or a whisk until stiff peaks form. Use a metal spoon to gently fold half the egg white into the batter and then fold in the remaining half. Spread the batter over the raspberries in the baking dish and place the dish in the larger baking dish. Pour boiling water in the larger dish until it reaches halfway up the sides, creating a bain marie. Transfer to the oven and bake for 40–50 minutes, until puffy and golden. Set aside for 10 minutes, dust with icing sugar and serve.

SERVES 4

Block of chocolate

I would never describe myself as having a really big sweet tooth, but chocolate doesn't count as a sweet, does it? I live with four girls, and chocolate is a mania in our home. We've been known to spend entire holidays searching for chocolate shops in every town we visit. I would like to say that I always keep a block in the house, but that has proved virtually impossible – two hours would be its maximum lifespan. My girls couldn't detect the pea under the pile of mattresses, but I reckon they could lie on the bed, eat the chocolate and confidently separate out the squares of 70% cocoa from the 85% cocoa. Does that classify my daughters as true princesses?

CINNAMON CHOCOLATE MOUSSE If you're in need of a chocolate fix but are too lazy to bother beating eggs, this is the dish for you: simple and gorgeous.

250g dark chocolate (70% cocoa), plus extra, shaved
250ml double cream
½ teaspoon ground cinnamon
250g crème fraîche
cocoa powder, to dust

Melt the chocolate in a metal mixing bowl placed over a saucepan of simmering water. Remove from heat and allow to cool. Whip the cream and cinnamon in a bowl with electric beaters until soft peaks just start to form, being careful not to reach firm peaks. Stir the crème fraîche into the melted chocolate, then fold in a third of the whipped cream. Follow with the remaining cream.

Spoon into serving bowls, sprinkle with the shaved chocolate, dust with cocoa and serve immediately.
SERVES 4

CHOCOLATE AND CHERRY TART Chocolate and cherries are perfect partners, both in poetic alliteration and in a case of shortcrust pastry.

125g unsalted butter, melted and cooled
80g caster sugar, plus 3 tablespoons extra
190g plain flour, plus 2 tablespoons extra
pinch sea salt
125ml single cream
2 small eggs, lightly beaten
2 teaspoons vanilla extract
75g good-quality dark chocolate, melted
2 tablespoons ground almonds
450g cherries, halved and pitted
icing sugar, to dust

Preheat the oven to 180°C/gas mark 4 and grease a 13cm x 35cm tart tin.

To make the pastry, stir together the butter and sugar in a large bowl. Add the flour and salt and stir to make a soft dough. Transfer to the tart tin and press the dough evenly into the base and sides with your fingertips. Cover and refrigerate for 30 minutes minimum.

Place the tart tin on a baking tray and bake for 15 minutes, or until the pastry is golden and lightly puffy. Meanwhile, to make the filling, whisk together the cream, egg, vanilla extract, melted chocolate and the extra caster sugar. Add the extra plain flour and whisk until well combined. Remove the tart tin from the oven and sprinkle the ground almonds over the pastry base. Pour the filling evenly over the top and poke in the cherries. Bake in the oven for a further 25 minutes, or until the filling is just firm.

Allow the tart to cool before removing it from the tin. Dust with icing sugar to serve. **SERVES 4**

FLOURLESS CHOCOLATE CAKE This is so dense it's more a dessert than a cake. Serve with a strong black coffee and you'll be kick-started back to life.

300g good-quality dark
  chocolate, chopped
180g unsalted butter,
  cut into pieces
6 large eggs, separated
165g caster sugar
2 teaspoons vanilla extract
cocoa powder, to dust
double cream, to serve

Preheat the oven to 180°C/gas mark 4. Butter a 22cm-diameter spring form tin and line the base and sides with greaseproof paper.

Stir together the chocolate and butter in a small saucepan over low heat until smooth. Remove from heat and stir occasionally until cooled to lukewarm.

Beat the egg yolks and half the sugar with electric beaters until thick and pale. Fold the lukewarm chocolate through the mixture, then fold in the vanilla extract. Using clean beaters and a separate bowl, beat the egg whites until soft peaks form. Gradually add the remaining sugar until medium peaks form. Fold a third of the whites into the chocolate and then fold in the remaining whites. Pour the batter into the lined tin.

Bake for 35–40 minutes, or until a skewer inserted into the centre comes out with moist crumbs. Leave to cool in the pan on a cake rack. Transfer to a serving plate and dust with cocoa. Serve with a bowl of combined cream and cocoa. **SERVES 8**

HOT MARSHMALLOW FUDGE SUNDAES My family is obsessed with camping and toasting marshmallows over the fire. This is a good way to use any leftovers (if you have them) and cheer everyone up when you arrive home to real life.

250ml double cream
180g good-quality dark
  chocolate, chopped
1 teaspoon cocoa powder,
  plus extra to dust
100g marshmallows
vanilla and chocolate ice-cream
50g roasted hazelnuts,
  skinned and halved

Place the cream in a small saucepan over medium heat and bring to a simmer. Remove from heat, add the chocolate and cocoa and mix until smooth and glossy. Return to low heat, add the marshmallows and stir gently until they start to melt.

Scoop the ice-cream into serving bowls and drizzle over the hot fudge and marshmallow sauce. Scatter with the hazelnuts and dust lightly with cocoa.

SERVES 4

CHOCOLATE CHUNK MERINGUE CAKE Gooey melted chocolate and crunchy pistachios come together in this free-form chewy meringue. If eating it gives you palpitations of guilt, throw some berries on top and kid yourself it's a fruit dessert.

6 egg whites
220g golden caster sugar
200g good-quality dark
  chocolate, roughly chopped
100g pistachio nuts, roughly
  chopped, plus extra to decorate
300ml double cream

Preheat the oven to 160°C/gas mark 3. Draw a 26cm-diameter circle on a length of baking paper, turn it over so the marks are underneath and place the paper on a large oven tray.

In a clean bowl whisk the egg whites with electric beaters until soft peaks form. Add the sugar 1 tablespoon at a time, whisking well between each addition, until all the sugar is incorporated. Fold through the chocolate and pistachios. Transfer to the baking paper and spread out, keeping the mixture roughly inside the circle.

Bake for 1 hour or until cooked through. Cool thoroughly. Beat the cream to soft peaks, spread over the meringue and scatter with extra pistachios.

SERVES 8

'This looks impressive, but is difficult to mess up –
perfect recipe credentials, as far as I'm concerned.
It isn't a true Aussie pavlova, but I always think a
light meringue dessert is great after a fancy meal.'

Index

FOR NATALIE, EDIE, INÈS, BUNNY and anyone who has ever tried to get a good meal on the table after 6pm… It's been an enormous year. I've completed this book, opened a restaurant in London and one in central Tokyo, taken on a weekly column in the *Independent on Sunday,* 'The New Review', as well as my regular writing for various magazines. I've had a daughter start a new school and we've acquired a very big black Labrador called Skippy. There's a passionate team of very loyal people helping me get all this done so that I can still get dinner on the table each night for my family. So an enormous thank you firstly to Lou D, who has joined me this year and has helped organise me and my work – no mean feat; Erika and Mikkel, you make me feel calm and reassured, and your combined vision and energy fuels the furnace for all of us, even on this my 10th book; Glenda for polishing and enhancing my words; Jane Price for her sense of humour and insight, even into my own condition; Victoria for her organisation, experience and support; my book food team Lou M, Nick and Rosie – where would I be without your commitment, wealth of knowledge and attention to detail? These days I'd rather a new plate to a new shirt, so thank you to Geraldine and the fortynine for working together to produce such unique and beautiful ceramic pieces; Klint for being everything to everyone and an appreciative taste tester; Paul Aikman for his eye for colour and taking our images that extra 10 per cent; Antony for his sensible and sensitive guidance; Lizzy for her confidence and enthusiasm; Sylvia, who is always there for us; Natalie for being my partner in crime, and finally, to my family, who show me the exquisite joy that cooking and looking after others can bring.

Creative Director: Erika Oliveira
Photograper: Mikkel Vang
Art Director: Louise Davids
Editor: Glenda Downing
Contributing Editor: Jane Price
Food Stylist: Lou Mackaness
Food preparation: Nick Banbury
Recipe testing: Rosie Reynolds
Prop Stylist: Geraldine Muñoz
Photography Assistant: Klint Collier
Production Manager: Victoria Jefferys
Prepress: Paul Aikman, Graphic Print Group
Producer: Natalie Elliott

For Collins:
Editorial Director: Lizzy Gray
Senior Project Editor: Georgina Atsiaris
Production: Anna Mitchelmore

The publisher, Bill Granger and the creative team would like to sincerely thank the following for their generosity in assistance with kitchenware, homewares and clothes: Aeria Tiles, Bassike, Bisanna Tiles, Mud Australia, Jac and Jack, Jon Mullens, Major and Tom, Miele and Prop Stop.

A special thanks to the fortynine and Sandy Lockwood for their beautiful handcrafted ceramic pieces.

the fortynine: page 2, 5, 6, 14-15, 18, 24, 33, 34, 37, 52, 59, 69, 70-71, 93, 97, 105, 138, 140, 143, 144-145, 146, 152, 160, 163, 164, 171, 172, 177, 180, 183, 184, 187, 188, 194, 200, 206-207,, 219, 222, 230, 235, 236

Sandy Lockwood: page 5, 26, 39, 49, 60, 70-71, 75, 114, 144-145, 158, 171, 183, 187, 222

And finally a big thank you to Rachel Jukes, Tamin Jones and Lucy Heeley for their additional work on the UK edition.

First published in 2012 by Collins,
an imprint of HarperCollinsPublishers

77–85 Fulham Palace Road
Hammersmith
London, W6 8JB
www.harpercollins.co.uk

10 9 8 7 6 5 4 3 2 1

Text © 2012 William Granger
Photography © 2012 Mikkel Vang
Design and layout © 2012 bills Licensing Pty Limited

A catalogue record of this book is available
from the British Library.

ISBN 978-0-00-747822-4

Printed and bound by South China Printing Company Ltd

www.bills.com.au

All spoon measures are level unless otherwise stated and 1 tablespoon equals 15ml. Cooking temperatures and times relate to conventional ovens. If you are using a fan-assisted oven, set the oven temperature 20 degrees lower. For baking, I recommend a conventional oven rather than a fan-assisted oven.

Anyone who is pregnant or in a vulnerable health group should consult their doctor regarding eating raw or lightly cooked eggs.